BECOMING THE
PERSON
YOU WANT TO BE

DISCOVERING YOUR
DIGNITY AND WORTH

D1538540

BECOMING THE PERSON YOU WANT TO BE

DISCOVERING YOUR DIGNITY AND WORTH

DR. JAMES B. RICHARDS

BECOMING THE PERSON YOU WANT TO BE
Discovering Your Dignity and Worth

ISBN 978-0-924748-34-9
UPC 885713000048

Printed in the United States of America
© 2004 by Dr. James B. Richards

MileStones International Publishers
P.O. Box 104
Newburg, PA 17240
(303) 503-7257
www.milestonesintl.com

3 4 5 6 7 8 9 10 11 / 11

DEDICATION

It is the quality of our friendships that determine the quality of our lives. Great friends are rare, and lifelong friends are a treasure. My life's accomplishments are as much the investment of my friends as they are of my own efforts. It is, after all, my friends who played such a major role in influencing my life to become the person I am today.

In loving appreciation for a heart-connection that has endured for a large part of our lives, Brenda and I dedicate this book to two of the greatest friends we have ever known. Don and Edwina McCaslin, thank you.

CONTENTS

INTRODUCTION: THE KEY

We all know the many promises Jesus made in God's Word. When we commit our lives to Christ, we come to the Kingdom of God hoping, expecting our lives to be different, and in many ways they are. Dramatically different! Yet we still seem to struggle to actually live our dreams. We initially make some headway, but then we stall out in our Christian walk.

Entropy is a law of physics that says anything left to itself will tend toward disorganization. This same law that works in the natural world also works in the realm of the heart. Jesus used the laws of nature to help us understand the laws of the heart. The apostle Paul said, *"For since the creation of the world His invisible attributes are clearly seen, being understood by the things that are made, even His eternal power and Godhead"* (Romans 1:20).

Based on this spiritual law and dozens of other scriptural examples, if we are not investing in our life it falls apart. I think we all know that. I believe most people are doing all they know to do to improve their personal character and the quality of their lives. The fact that you've picked up this book says you are someone who is serious about personal development. You are not willing to settle. You want all that Jesus died to give you.

Over twenty-five years ago, I developed what I now call the Law of Personal Investment. I made some decisions about investing in my life that brought dramatic transformation. I had always had a good prayer life. Since the time I accepted Jesus, I have always read my Bible. I studied the Word as a serious disciple. But, as I walked with God, I learned that just spending time doing things from a serious heart was not enough. The old adage "practice makes perfect" is actually misleading. According to Tony Robbins, a leader in the field of personal coaching, practice doesn't make perfect…it just makes permanent!

If you practice your golf swing improperly, you don't improve. In fact, you usually get worse. I know musicians who practice every day, but they don't improve. Their practice sessions are spent playing the same songs they already know, the same way they've always played them. They don't improve because they don't know how to practice in a way that brings personal development.

You may be new to the world of personal investment, but I would bet that almost every person who picks up this book has tried a lot of things. You have been diligent, but you have not gotten the results you expected. You now realize that the amount of time you put into personal development is no indicator of your return. You are now asking new questions like, "How do I make the kind of life investments that would really reap the kinds of results I want to see?" You are looking for the "key"!

My good friend Ron McIntosh, director of Victory Bible Institute in Tulsa, Oklahoma, recently shared an example that I thought addressed this issue perfectly. In a leadership meeting he gave a staff member a key and asked her to go outside the room. The door was locked behind her.

At the appropriate time she was to use the key to re-enter the room.

At the designated signal she attempted to unlock the door. She vainly struggled to enter the room, but the door would not open! She persisted in her efforts. She even called out for help, but all to no avail. The door would not open. Then he asked the leaders attending the lecture, "What should she have done? Should she have tried harder? Should she have tried longer? Did she have enough faith? Did she really want to get back in the room?" Finally he said, "None of those things would have helped." He finally revealed, "She had the wrong key."

Then he continued to explain that as leaders we have assumed people didn't really want to move forward. We have blamed their lack of faith. We have questioned their commitment. We have told them they needed to try harder, pray more, cry out to God, and a plethora of other "spiritual gymnastics." But the truth is we have never given them the right key.

No matter how sincere you are, no matter how hard you try, without the right key you will not open the door to the life you want, the life God promised, the life Jesus died to give you. In this book, I will give you what I believe is the key. It's not a mystery, and it's not difficult. In fact, it's so simple that we've overlooked it, scoffed at it, and tried every other approach. I will take you back to the very fundamentals of Christianity. I will introduce you to the secret key to positive, painless, permanent, effortless change!

This is not a philosophical idea conjured up at my desk as I searched for sermon material. The key I will share with you is a reflection of my personal journey with God. It was forged in the crucible of my life and proven through thirty years of ministry. Thousands of desperate and struggling people have applied this to their lives. Business people have used this key to move forward in their businesses and careers. Ministers have employed this tool to break through to the next level of growth. Untold numbers of men and women have used this principle to become the kind of spouse that builds a loving marriage.

Just as thousands of others have used this key to open the door to their future, you too can open the door before you. You can be the person you want to be. And the journey will be an incredible, exciting, enjoyable adventure!

CHAPTER ONE

THE POSITIVE POWER OF DESIRE

The young man and his wife were new to my church. Much of their short Christian experience had been spent in a church that didn't embrace the promises of God. Instead of learning about Jesus' promises to meet our needs and satisfy our longings, they had been led to believe that refusing their natural and normal desires was some sort of obligatory proof of their love for God.

"I'm such a bad person," the young husband insisted repeatedly. It took most of the first hour to get him to pinpoint what exactly made him think so poorly of himself. "I just lust after so many things," he reluctantly admitted. When he jumped out of his seat, I thought he was going to run out the door. Instead he began to pace the floor. Apparently the strain of his confession was more than he could manage while sitting still.

In a flash, his sorrow turned to anger. "I want things!" he angrily declared as he paced my office floor. His statement expressed a deep frustration. Then he spun on his heels, leaned across my desk to look me in the eye, and declared, "And I don't care what you think about it!"

"I think you should have things," I announced in response. He stared at me with stunned surprise. I continued, "As a matter of fact, the Bible says that God knows you have need of things. And as long as you keep Him first in your life, He actually promises to fulfill your heart's desires."

He froze. His gaze was locked onto mine. He wrinkled his forehead as if to momentarily consider this concept. But it was too foreign for him. Before he could even grasp this truth, he began to defend the wrong doctrine that had created his situation and brought him to my office in the first place.

When I finally calmed him down, I began to explain, "Desire can be the most positive or the most destructive force in your life. It can cause you to wrap your life around God, or it can cause you to abandon God. It can be the first step toward temptation or the first step toward faith. Desire becomes an incredibly positive power when you know God wants to meet your needs and fulfill your desires." The counseling session ended with a homework assignment to look at the scriptures in the New Testament that spoke of desire and promises.

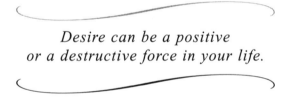

Desire can be a positive
or a destructive force in your life.

This young man's hunger for fulfillment soon led him on a quest for God that was beyond anything he had ever known. When God became his true source of provision, his entire life changed dramatically. When he discovered that Jesus had died to make all of the promises of God available to him, his love and appreciation for God multiplied. A peace, love, and gratefulness overtook his anger. His desires never again took him away from God. They took him full force toward God as his only source for the fulfillment of all of his needs and desires.

Market research tells us there are a few clear-cut things that nearly everybody wants. We all actually want the same things. We want to be happy, healthy, and prosperous and have loving relationships. Problems arise, however, when we look around and see the gap between what we desire and what we are experiencing. We then struggle to explain that gap based on our spiritual beliefs or background.

For some who are caught in this struggle, life becomes total disillusionment. Hopeless people see no possibilities of reaching their dreams. They see no way to fill the void between what they have and what they want. The realization comes that something must change in order for them to reach their goals. Some honestly believe that in order for them to get what they themselves want, everyone around them must change. So they set about to take charge of everyone else's life while their own lives spin further out of control. Still others feel threatened by the thought that they themselves may have to change to reach their goals.

In reality, the idea of personal change, as ominous as it may be, holds the only legitimate hope of fulfillment. Many people shrink back from the challenge of change. It looks too frightening or difficult. Other people, though, forge ahead with reckless abandonment toward their goals, ready to pay the ultimate price of personal change in order to live their dreams. What is it that motivates these people to overcome the threat of change? The answer is simple: desire!

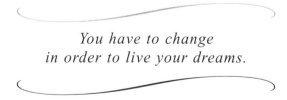

You have to change
in order to live your dreams.

But where do these determined people find such strong desire? The secret is in their expectation of positive benefits.

That's right! The expectation of fulfillment, satisfaction, and pleasure causes an increase in desire. These people are willing to pay the price of any challenge to reach their desired goals. Their expectations create a desire that is so strong that nothing will deter them from their course.

So how can we know when we have enough desire to carry us the distance to our dreams? I've heard the answer to that question in an ancient Eastern story about a man who sought enlightenment. He spent years trying to find someone who could help him in his search. Eventually he heard of a sage who lived alone as a monk. When the hungry seeker located the monk he found him meditating by a stream. He rushed to him and pleaded, "Will you help me? I seek enlightenment." To his utter amazement, the old monk grabbed his head and pushed it under the water.

After what seemed an eternity the old monk pulled the man's head up from the water. With the first breath, the seeker began complaining, "What are you doing? I just want you to show me how to find...." Before he could finish his statement the old monk simply pushed his head back under water and held it for an even longer time. Once again, when the man's head emerged, with his first breath he fussed, complained, and argued. The third time the monk pushed his head under water and held it until the seeker thought he would drown.

When his soaked head emerged from the water, the seeker simply gasped for breath. He had no thought of his complaints and arguments. He just filled his lungs with refreshing air. Then the old monk calmly said, "When you desire enlightenment as badly as you wanted that breath of air, you will find it."

When we want something more than we want anything else, we will find it whatever the cost. God said it this way: *"And you will seek Me and find Me, when you search for Me with all your heart"* (Jeremiah 29:13). When our desire is strong, we are highly motivated. We overcome obstacles. We refuse to become sidetracked by the many distractions, no matter how legitimate. We are determined. We will not be denied! We succeed in finding the things we desire when we seek them passionately. All else becomes a trivial pursuit.

Most of us, however, are conditioned to choosing a lifestyle in which we have the greatest amount of pleasure and the least amount of pain. It is called settling! There are things we wish we had, but our conditioning keeps us from seeking them. There are things we know we need, but habitual choices prevent us from attaining them. There are even things we have adapted to that cause us pain and guilt, but our fear of change keeps us from finding deliverance from the situation.

Many times life steals our passion. We are like the proverbial frog in the pot. Every day the heat gets turned up a little until we are being cooked and don't even realize it. We relinquish our dreams to the limitations defined by our experience. We lose our uniqueness to the rules of society. We surrender our destiny to a dwarfed sense of self. We are so caught up in the grind of living, like the frog in the pot, that we surrender more of our lives to mediocrity every day and don't realize it.

In this mundane maze, our goals are reduced to dreams, our dreams are diminished to wishes, and our wishes melt away into fantasies. Then one day we put away our fantasies and accept what we falsely call "real life." We are alive, but our dreams are dead! Our bodies go through the motions of daily activity while our hearts ache for fulfillment.

If this describes you, it's not too late. To recover your life, the first thing you've got to do is resurrect your desire. Let yourself dream again. Use your imagination to consider all the pleasure and fulfillment that waits in the realization of your dreams. Accept the fact that God wants you to live your dreams while walking with Him! In fact, God wants us to dream! Part of His purpose for taking us through transformation is so that we can live our dreams.

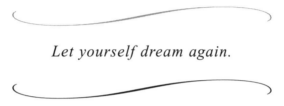

Let yourself dream again.

The prophet Joel spoke of a day when *"old men shall dream dreams"* (Joel 2:28). That day is now. The Holy Spirit has been poured out. If you are washed in the blood of Jesus, then His Spirit is in you and upon you. The Holy Spirit will restore your dreams and give you the power to live them, regardless of how old you are!

To resurrect your passion you must recover some of your dreams. So where do you start? You don't start by clearly identifying your ultimate dreams. You begin simply by recognizing the things in your life that are not as you would have them. Then you must define how you want them to be. Once you have a picture of what you want, then allow yourself to experience the expectations of positive results.

Here's a step-by-step process that will lead you away from disillusionment and into the fulfillment of your desires.

1. Make a list of ten things in your life with which you are not satisfied.

2. Make a list of all the pain, suffering, or sorrow in your life as a result of this diminished lifestyle.

3. Make a list of how you would have those things to be if there were no limitations.

4. Make a long list of as many benefits as you can think of that you believe these changes would bring to your life, your happiness, your personal peace, your relationships with others, and your relationship with God.

5. Make sure your list of benefits is at least twice as long as the list of pain and problems. The longer the better!

6. Imagine what it would be like to enjoy those benefits. Try to come to the place where you would know what it actually feels like to experience the benefits.

7. Ponder this until you feel passion to have those benefits in your life, even if it takes days or weeks. First thing in the morning and last thing at night is the best time to think on these things. See and feel yourself enjoying the benefits of these changes.

8. Acknowledge to God that you know He wants you to have the best.

9. Affirm to yourself that reading this book and taking the suggested steps are essential to getting you where you want to go.

10. Make a decision that you will seek until you find.

CHAPTER TWO

DISCOVERING YOUR DESTINY

When a person has a sense of destiny, his entire world looks and feels different. He is motivated and, consequently, a more positive person. His problems become little more than speed bumps on the road of purpose. Obstacles are viewed as challenges. He is more physically energetic. His sense of destiny provides him with the encouragement and the parameters essential for a healthy productive life. He has a strong vision of his future.

Vision is imperative in the quest for fulfillment. Proverbs 29:18 says, *"Where there is no vision, the people run wild"* (MLB). The New International Version says it like this: *"Where there is no revelation, the people cast off restraint."* Regardless of how you say it, or what translation you use, people who have no sense of destiny flounder without direction. They struggle with the motivation essential for life. Discouragement comes easily. Setbacks are plentiful. Life is hard. The lack of a clear-cut destination undermines every effort, making any aspect of life more difficult.

Some people have a very clearly defined sense of destiny. They know where they are going. They have a destination in mind. Their life is a mission. Others do not. If this is you, don't despair. Regardless of where you are in this process, you can develop a clear sense of destiny. And you can transform your ability to live your destiny. God has provided all of us with a starting place to develop an incredible sense of divine purpose. Although many struggle trying to find this starting place, you don't have to be among them. Today can be the day that launches you into a divine destiny. The information in this chapter alone has changed the course of life for thousands. Let me tell you of one such person who had to deal with this issue.

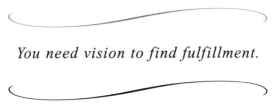

You need vision to find fulfillment.

Greg was a man who liked details. This was a great strength in his work. In fact, he was probably the best detail man that his company had ever employed. He often won awards related to his ability to work with details. But like any strength, when it was overused it worked against him.

When Greg would bring his attention to detail into other areas of his life, it complicated simple issues. He would often experience what is commonly called the "paralysis of analysis." To put it in simple terms, Greg got stuck—a lot. If he didn't have all the details, he sometimes became agitated, confused, and angry. His walk with God sometimes bogged down as a result of his need for excessive information.

Greg found my emphasis on developing an intimate relationship with God to be overly simplistic and frustrating. He wanted more details. He thought details would solve his problem and settle his fears.

He was especially agitated the day he came for his appointment. He had a sudden burst of emotion that was very unlike him. Normally, he was poised and diplomatic. I knew he must be close to the edge when he blurted out, "Why doesn't God just come right out and say, 'This is your destiny'? It would make life so simple!"

Although he was very competent in his work, Greg was struggling with feelings of inadequacy. He still had no sense of destiny or direction, and he was tormented with not knowing. After months of being in our church and going through much of the foundational training we offer, he was still dissatisfied. I had the task of helping him see that his dissatisfaction grew out of a refusal to make the decisions before him. He was sure that there were other things he needed to know and that God should be responsible enough to tell him!

As a pastor with over thirty years of ministry experience, I've seen this situation hundreds of times. Greg was stuck in one place. He didn't know what to do with his life. And he wanted specific direction from God. He felt unsafe taking any steps until he had all the steps; therefore, he took no steps. He was stagnant. The lack of forward movement brought an incredible sense of dissatisfaction. He often found himself angry toward those who felt a clear sense of purpose and destiny.

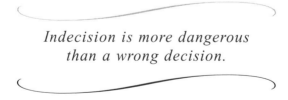

*Indecision is more dangerous
than a wrong decision.*

Although I had given him the information he needed, it was not what he wanted. Like many Christians, he felt he knew more than God did about how he should be led. But I assured him that God's plan was always best. I advised him to act on what he knew and then what he needed to know would evolve from the process.

Greg didn't realize the torment of doing nothing. He was so afraid of making a wrong decision that he made no decision. Once again, by not trusting God's wisdom, he created more pain with his indecision than he would have had with a wrong decision. In 1 Kings 18:21, Elijah said to the people, *"How long will you falter between two opinions?"* We sometimes fail to see the danger of indecision. A wrong decision can be corrected. Indecision offers no hope, no relief, and no opportunities for redirection.

Moses challenged the people of Israel when he said:

For this commandment which I command you today, it is not too mysterious for you, nor is it far off. It is not in heaven, that you should say, "Who will ascend into heaven for us and bring it to us, that we may hear it and do it?" Nor is it beyond the sea, that you should say, "Who will go over the sea for us and bring it to us, that we may hear it and do it?" But the word is very near you, in your mouth and in your heart, that you may do it (Deuteronomy 30:11-14).

He was making it clear! God's Word is not that mysterious and difficult. We don't need special revelations. We just need to decide based on what we know about God. In verse 19, Moses continued:

I call heaven and earth as witnesses today against you, that I have set before you life and death, blessing and cursing; therefore choose life, that both you and your descendants may live.

As I shared with Greg these scriptures about making decisions, he insisted that he did not know what he should decide.

At this point I took him to a scripture that I often share with those who have no sense of destiny: *"For whom He foreknew, He also predestined to be conformed to the image of His Son"* (Romans 8:29). This scripture is the starting place to discover destiny. Most people attempt to understand their destiny by discovering what they desire to do. However, our destiny is not in what we will do; it is in who we will become! Becoming is far more important than doing! If you become who you should be, you can only do what you should do!

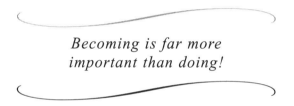

*Becoming is far more
important than doing!*

God predestined the heart of our personal destiny. He embedded what we would do in the process of our personal development. Becoming is our ultimate purpose! He wants us all to be like Jesus. In other words, it is our destiny to change, to grow, to become more like Jesus! This is the journey of our life. This should be our continual pursuit. As we become who God would have us to be, then what we should do becomes obvious.

At this point, Greg insisted that he still did not have enough information. But he really did. The question was not, do you have enough information? The real question was, do you trust the information you have? Are you willing to act on it? Are you willing to follow God with your whole heart? Are you willing to put personal development ahead of the quest for information? Are you willing to become the person God wants you to be in order to discover what God wants you to do?

Answer the following questions as honestly as you can. As you deal with your personal issues, commit yourself to a life of becoming more like Jesus. Don't worry about how you will do it. Just make the commitment to take each step as it becomes known to you.

1. Do you believe God wants to make you more like Jesus?

2. Have you fully committed yourself to a life of personal development?

3. How can you act on what you already know about God's will for your life?

4. Make a list of five steps you will take to develop your personal life.

5. Make a list of all the good things that would happen in your life if you were more like Jesus.

6. Make a list of some negative situations that would disappear if you were more like Jesus.

Chapter Three

The Power to Become

Jesus walked up to a crippled man and said, "Stand up and walk!" The crippled man could have said, "Don't You see that I am crippled? Heal me and I will walk." God's grace always takes us beyond the limits of *our* power and ability and ushers us into *His* realm of power and ability. But, like the cripple, we must be willing to do what we can not do.

Nearly everybody struggles with the idea of change because they know they do not have the power to change. They have tried and failed, made resolution, done everything within their power, and often find themselves struggling with the same issues. If you've tried everything you know to change and have failed...good! Now that you know you can't, you're free to move on to understanding how Christ in you can change you.

Just walk into any bookstore in America, and you will see the evidence that America is in the midst of a self-improvement craze. People want help! Self-help books and motivational programs have become the rage of the nation. Millions of dollars are spent every year by people who are seeking to become the person they want to be.

Yet, one look at the statistics tells us that very little improvement is taking place. Crime is on the rise. Road rage, school murders, and all conceivable violations of human dignity seem to be increasing. Religious groups who claim to have the answers are murdering one another in the name of their god. Even Christians seem to be facing many of the same relational and emotional issues as non-Christians. So, if everyone is trying so hard to improve, why isn't it getting better? Why do people get good information and have such difficulty changing?

The answer is simple! Information and empowerment are not the same thing. I believe in the virtue of learning. But learning has become the stumbling block of Western culture. We have exalted knowing over doing or being. But knowledge causes frustration when we can't come up with the means to implement what we know. Self-help only works to the degree that one can help oneself. It is dependent on personal power and self-control. All the self-help materials in the world have one basic flaw: They only work for those who already have a high degree of personal strength and character. So, while some see a bit of improvement, most of us only get frustrated and disillusioned by our inability to make the information work to any significant degree.

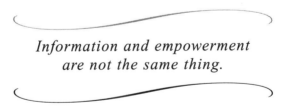

Information and empowerment
are not the same thing.

This is not a new problem. We can find evidence of the same thing in the Old Testament. The prophet Jeremiah asked this question, *"Can the Ethiopian change his skin or the leopard its spots? Neither can you do good who are accustomed to doing evil"* (Jeremiah 13:23, NIV). This question has been asked since the dawn of civilization: "Can people really change?" This has been debated for centuries by the greatest minds of the world. Great philosophers, educators, and world-renowned religious leaders have said that knowledge and education could change man. But I will humbly offer a simple, yet scriptural, perspective: Apart from God's help, people can only change to the degree that they have personal strength.

God looked at mankind and his inability to rise above his level of personal power. He desired to make all of His promises sure to every human being. But this would be impossible if it depended on each person's ability. The people who needed the greatest amount of change were the people who had the least ability.

In Romans 4:16 Paul wrote, *"Therefore it is of faith that it might be according to grace, so that the promise might be sure to all the seed."* God gave every person a measure of faith.[1] He made sure we had enough faith to trust Him. He embedded the seed of faith in us at creation. Then He sent Jesus, who brought grace and truth to ensure that we could all experience the power to change, regardless of our personal strength.

You see, information alone is never enough to bring about the kind of change and growth that most of us desire. Information, regardless of how true it is, cannot empower a person to change. Consider the Old Testament. It was true. In fact, it was incredible truth. It provided mankind with the wisdom of God for living on this planet. Moses brought

---

1. Ephesians 2:8: *"For by grace you have been saved through faith, and that not of yourselves; it is the gift of God, not of works, lest anyone should boast."* See also Romans 12:3.

truth.[2] The Old Testament was truth. It was an incredible self-help system. It gave us rules and principles for healthy living. It gave us the guidelines for great relationships. It gave us the blueprint for a national economic system that worked. It was the basis of the American judicial system. But it had one monumental weakness—people!

"For what the law could not do in that it was weak through the flesh, God did by sending His own Son" (Romans 8:3). The Law depended on people who depended on their strength—their flesh! If the principles of the Law given by God did not give man the power to change, it is doubtful that any self-help book can give us the power to change. So, what do we do? Are we left to flounder in our limitations? Not for a minute!

In our quest to change we have looked everywhere to find the answers. Science looks to the cosmos. Most Eastern religions and New Age teachings encourage man to find the resources within himself. To be honest I believe there is merit in connecting to our inner resources; however, these philosophical approaches have two basic flaws. First, they alienate man from the resources of God. And second, like the Law of Moses, they limit us to the extent of our personal strength. Even if they would work, they would only work for the strong. God loved us too much to leave us to our own resources. He wanted everyone to partake of His limitless provision!

While seeking the answers, we have blindly stepped over the solution. It was in front of us all the time, but we did not recognize it. It is like the story about the man who daily sat on a box begging. Every day he would drag his

---

2.   John 1:17: *"For the law was given through Moses, but grace and truth came through Jesus Christ."*

box out to the street, sit on it, and beg pennies from the passersby. After years of sitting on the box begging, someone asked him what was in the box. He had no idea. It was just a box he had found years before. It was the perfect height to sit on while begging. It had never occurred to him to look inside. When he finally decided to look in the box he discovered that it was full of money. There was more than enough money for him to have lived comfortably all his life.

We have a treasure[3] that we have never fully recognized. Like beggars sitting on a box of money, we have never discovered the treasure of God's grace.[4] Grace is God's ability, capacity, divine influence, and power that works from the heart and is given without merit. In other words, grace is God's ability to do what I do not have the ability to do. When Jesus came, He did not bring us simply the truth. He also brought what no religious leader, no prophet, and no self-help guru could bring. He brought us the ability and the power to live the truth and become who we were really created to be.

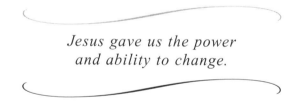

Jesus gave us the power
and ability to change.

Jesus lifts us beyond the limits of our personal capacity to change. He deposits within us the power of almighty God. All that God is, all that He can do, and all of His great

---

3.　2 Corinthians 4:7: *"But we have this treasure in earthen vessels, that the excellence of the power may be of God and not of us."*

4 .　To learn more, read my book, *Grace: The Power to Change* (New Kensington, Pennsylvania: Whitaker House, 1993).

power is in us—now! God gives this freely to everyone who accepts the gift of Jesus. Then He sends the Holy Spirit to live in us as our source of strength and power.

The apostle Paul made continual reference to the mystery of God that was being revealed in the New Covenant. In Colossians 1:25-27, he reveals the heart of this eternal mystery. This mystery holds the secret to personal empowerment. It is the treasure in the vessel.

> *I became a minister according to the stewardship from God which was given to me for you, to fulfill the word of God, the mystery which has been hidden from ages and from generations, but now has been revealed to His saints. To them God willed to make known what are the riches of the glory of this mystery among the Gentiles: which is Christ in you, the hope of glory.*

Christ in us is the hope of becoming the person we desire to be. In fact, Christ in us is the only sure hope for living our dreams to the fullest!

Christ is ready to flood our hearts with His strength. But we must prepare a place for Him. You can only put contents in an empty vessel. If the vessel is full, it does not have the capacity to hold anything else. It's like buying new clothes and bringing them home to a closet full of old worn-out clothes. If you don't get rid of the old, you have no room for the new.

*Depending on our own strength
keeps us from experiencing God's strength.*

Our hearts are full of the way we have done it. Our hearts are full of our own strength. Our dependence on our own strengths is the major obstacle to experiencing God's strength. The only way we can empty ourselves is by changing what we trust. When the Bible talks about dying to self, this is a major aspect of the process. As long as we continue to depend on self, to depend on our own strength, we can only achieve as far as our personal ability will take us.

Will you continue to trust your wisdom, your strength, and your point of view, or will you begin to trust God's wisdom, God's strength, and God's point of view?

To build a tall building you first have to dig a deep hole. This fact would seem strange to a person who had never seen a skyscraper. If you took him to the construction site of the tallest building in the world during the most essential part of the construction phase, he would not see steel being erected hundreds of stories above the ground. He would see people digging deep into the earth. It would make very little sense at first. But digging out a deep hole is the most essential part. A strong foundation for your building requires a deep hole. You must remove the earth and replace it with your foundation material. If the foundation is too shallow, the building will collapse.

Likewise, we need to dig out and discard all of the habits, rituals, and strengths that we have relied on in the past to move us forward. They do not have the strength to hold up the dream we are building. We must dig deep to empty ourselves out so that we can fill up with God, who is a stronger, surer foundation than what we could ever be in and of ourselves.

It may make very little sense to you to think all of your strengths that have brought you this far are the limiting factors in your life, but it is true. You must build a new foundation in your life. You must connect to God as your foundation and source of strength.

Your personal strength can enable you to do many things, but it cannot empower you to become something new. With God's grace, you have the power to become and do. You have this treasure in you, this source of limitless power. Now you are going to discover one of the ultimate secrets for accessing that power.

Answer the following questions to begin digging out your self in order to lay a new foundation with God.

1. If you had unlimited personal power, what would you do that you are not doing now?

2. How would that make your life better?

3. Do you really know how to access God's power that is within you?

4. What steps will you take to make a place for God's power?

5. Make a list to describe how you will be and feel as you access the unlimited power of God.

CHAPTER FOUR

THE PARADOX OF BECOMING

We all long to become something! Our sense of destiny inspires us to look to the future for our divine role. On the one hand, this sense of destiny can be a positive aspiration that leads us to positive growth. On the other hand, it can be a destructive force that undermines our every dream. We must understand the subtle laws of the heart to unlock the mystery of how our passion-to-become can work both positively and negatively.

Dave, a friend of mine, argued with everyone around him every week as he was challenged by the messages I was preaching. He tried to convince himself and others that he disagreed from a doctrinal standpoint with what I was saying. But the truth was that he was afraid. He was afraid of the challenge of personal growth. He turned what could have been a positive challenge into a destructive obstacle. What was meant for his good became his downfall.

Dave was missing the truth of Proverbs 10:29 in his life. This scripture says, *"The way of the Lord is strength for the up-right."* The word *upright* literally means "straight." Those whose hearts are aligned with God's truth benefit from truth. Those whose hearts twist the truth are destroyed by it. Our reaction to truth is always an expression of our sense of self.

According to the laws of Heart Physics®,[5] the same laws that govern nature reveal aspects of how God works in our hearts. For example, in physics, the law of opposite force says that for every action there is an equal and opposite reaction. This same law works in the heart. While our desires may be positive, at the same time, our words may be subtly communicating something negative and destructive to our hearts.

Truth benefits your heart
when your heart is aligned with truth.

Dave continually spoke in negative words, which created a destructive reaction in his life. He thought the challenge to grow and develop was a challenge to *become*. His continual negativity made him focus on his lack or inability rather than on his possibilities.

By speaking negatively about the changes we want to make or about the process, we essentially end up convincing ourselves to not even make the effort. Oddly enough, because of our lack of understanding the paradox of becoming, we kill off a process that has already been completed for us.

Before getting saved, we long to become something new, something different. That desire drives us to look to God for the power to change. However, when we accept Jesus that phase of the quest ends. We have become something new!

Therefore, if anyone is in Christ, he is a new creation; old things have passed away; behold, all things have become new (2 Corinthians 5:17).

---

1.   Go to www.heartphysics.com to learn more.

This is not a mere cliché. It is an essential reality. It is the foundation of all New Testament life!

Immediately upon salvation we should begin to renew our mind. Now that we have become a new creation, we need to come to see ourselves in this new identity. This may be the single greatest violation that happens to new converts. They are not established in the fundamentals of the Christian faith. They are not told that they are a new creation. They think they simply had their sins forgiven. They are excited. They feel the love of God. And they are ready to do anything and everything that would be essential to pleasing God. Too often all that zeal, all that positive energy is misdirected! They are passionately set on a course of destruction before they take their first steps.

Through our Foundations of the Faith program,[2] we attempt to establish people in the fundamentals of the Christian life. Setting a person on the right course is essential for a life of victory! The sooner this happens, the less likely they are to fall into the trap of trying to become.

At the new birth, you need to know: 1) Your sins have been forgiven, 2) You have been given the gift of righteousness, 3) You are qualified for all that God has provided for you. The old you has died! If you continue to see yourself the way you have in the past, you will experience little benefit from what God has done in you. Your primary objective is to change the way you see yourself. Renewing your mind is the key, the starting place, the foundation of Christian living. It is the place where you begin to see yourself as a new

---

2.   To obtain this program, contact Impact International Publications, 3300 N. Broad Place, Huntsville, AL 35805, or by logging on to www. impactministries.com.

creation. You leave the realm of *becoming* and enter the place of *being.*

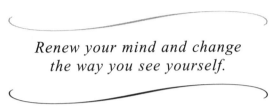

*Renew your mind and change
the way you see yourself.*

Those who are not introduced to the concept of renewing the mind think they still need to change. They are pursuing change more passionately than ever. They are, however, unwittingly operating the Heart Physics® law of reaction. The more they say to themselves, "I need to change," the more they believe they have not changed. The deeper their desire to become, the more deeply they believe they are not becoming! The genuine passion to live a life pleasing to God often becomes a trap that has no escape. As Isaiah the prophet said, *"My people have gone into captivity, because they have no knowledge"* (Isaiah 5:13).

Dave was desperate to please God. Unfortunately, he had zeal without knowledge. God can only be pleased by faith.[3] Faith is a trust in God's finished work. Rather than accepting what was already done for him, Dave was trying to become. Therefore, he reinforced the lie that he was not already transformed.

People who are properly introduced to the concept of renewing their mind realize that the change has already taken place. They are no longer trying to become. They have entered the realm of "I am!" They're not seeking to change.

---

3.   Hebrews 11:6: *"But without faith it is impossible to please Him, for he who comes to God must believe that He is, and that He is a rewarder of those who diligently seek Him."*

They are, however, seeking the transformation that comes as they see themselves in light of God's transforming power.

Although this concept of transformation versus change is subtle, it is essential to emotional and spiritual health. Change says, "I am not, and I must become." Transformation says, "I am, and I am yielding to a process." One contributes to faith and self-worth. The other tends toward unbelief and works-centered righteousness! One takes you to the place of rest. The other takes you to the place of continual effort and dead works. One produces righteousness consciousness. The other leads to sin consciousness! As subtle as the differences may seem, the consequences are enormous.

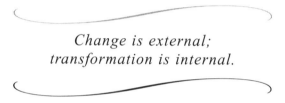

Change is external;
transformation is internal.

Change is external. Transformation is internal. Change comes from pressure. Most people who are trying to change are negatively motivated. They are assessing what's wrong with themselves and seeking to fix it. They feel pressured to change. People who are yielded to the process of transformation see who they really are in Jesus. They believe they have been made righteousness. They have of an image of themselves in Christ. Then they yield to the power of their new righteous nature. God's nature in them does the work.

This is so beyond the concepts of the natural mind. The natural mind says, "I *have* to change to please God." The spiritual mind says, "God's power is in me. I have become. I simply yield to His power that is at work in me." In the book of Romans, the apostle Paul introduced us to the plight of the person who thinks that his transformation is dependent on his own ability (flesh).

> *For those who live according to the flesh set their minds on the things of the flesh, but those who live according to the Spirit, the things of the Spirit. For to be carnally minded is death, but to be spiritually minded is life and peace. Because the carnal mind is enmity against God; for it is not subject to the law of God, nor indeed can be. So then, those who are in the flesh cannot please God* (Romans 8:5-9).

This is the perception of the person who has not renewed his mind. The way this person reasons makes it impossible for him to access God's limitless power. He is trapped in his own personal power. Although that may be adequate for some situations, it is never enough for all of life's challenges.

Romans 8:5-9 reads like this in *The Message*:

> *Those who think they can do it on their own end up obsessed with measuring their own moral muscle but never get around to exercising it in real life. Those who trust God's action in them find that God's Spirit is in them—living and breathing God! Obsession with self in these matters is a dead end; attention to God leads us out into the open, into a spacious, free life. Focusing on the self is the opposite of focusing on God. Anyone completely absorbed in self ignores God, ends up thinking more about self than God. That person ignores who God is and what he is doing. And God isn't pleased at being ignored.*

Can you image the frustration of trying as hard as you can to do and become the right thing, yet ignoring God the entire time; seeking to please God, yet living in a mind-set that makes it impossible? Paul said it like this when he described the Jews' earnest but self-centered approach to living for God:

> *For I can testify about them that they are zealous for God, but their zeal is not based on knowledge. Since they did not know the righteousness that comes from God and sought to establish their own, they did not submit to God's righteousness* (Romans 10:2-3, NIV).

Of all the destructive factors introduced into the life of a person obsessed with change, two prove to be the most deadly: 1) alienation from the power of God, and 2) the destruction of his sense of self-worth. When a person alienates himself from the power of God that is already in him, life remains a struggle with no or few victories. In the end, his entire relationship with God will be undermined. This in turn causes the destruction of his self-worth, which causes desire and passion to die.

Recognizing that change is already resident within you and then simply yielding to it will begin to release that person you've always dreamed you could be.

Here are a few exercises to help you picture yourself as the person you want to become.

1. Pick the top five character traits that you want to have in your life.

2. Write at least ten scriptures that describe some aspect of your new identity in Jesus.[4] Look for

---

4. If you want more than two hundred identity scriptures to use in your daily prayer life, go to www.impactministries.com and order *The Prayer Organizer*. It is an incredible tool for establishing a new sense of identity through prayer and worship.

scriptures that use the terms "in Him," "by Him," or "through Him."

3. Daily quote or think on these scriptures and affirm by saying, "This is who I am. Because I am in Christ, all of these characteristics are in me now! I am not becoming—I am!"

4. Begin to notice your self-talk. Be sure to change it to affirm your new identity in Christ.

5. If you have never invited Christ into your life, go to www.impactministries.com and click on the icon that says, "Would you like to know Jesus personally?" or call Impact Ministries at 256-536-9402. Ask to talk to someone who can introduce you to Jesus!

CHAPTER FIVE

FEELING RIGHT ABOUT ME

My friend Dave, whom I mentioned in the previous chapter, came in and out of my church for years. Every time I would preach something that was too challenging for him, he would blow out. He was so defensive that I could not help him see he was missing the point. Through the maze of his doctrinal arguments, he blinded himself to his real issues.

He was actually a good man. He loved God and wanted to grow. Yet, any time he was faced with a challenge in a new area, Dave took it to a negative place. We talked many times. Very seldom did he actually listen; he just came and argued his point.

Then, at a low point in his life, he finally admitted that he felt bad about himself. He struggled to feel like he measured up. He was suffering from low self-worth. Self-worth is one of the root issues of healthy human life. The Bible teaches that man at his creation was crowned with glory and honor, dignity and worth. Everything man was called to do on planet Earth on God's behalf was predicated by man's sense of God-given self-worth. If man does not feel right about himself, he will twist every positive challenge into a negative experience.

Making the journey of transformation depends upon having a positive, Bible-based sense of self-worth. In fact, successfully making the journey of life also depends upon it. No part of life can be experienced to its fullest, no aspect of walking with God or reaching personal goals can be completely realized without this essential self-perspective. Positive, Bible-based, God-centered self-worth is essential for every aspect of emotional and spiritual health.

Apart from being born again, the greatest need we have is the need for self-worth. The absence of self-worth is a breeding ground for every imaginable evil.[1] Rob someone of his self-worth and you will have stolen his future! Getting born again should be the beginning of a journey in dignity and worth. Every aspect of coming to know God should have

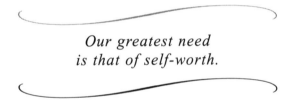

Our greatest need
is that of self-worth.

a positive effect on our sense of self! In fact, our self-worth is the key to our capacity to fulfill our God-given destiny.

The need to change is challenging. It is a testament to the fact that we are not "all right" and it explains the desperate search for answers that so many people undertake. When learning to win people to Jesus, we have been taught that we have to get them lost before we can get them saved, meaning that we begin our witnessing by attempting to convince them that they are sinners. Although it's true that we are born with a sin nature, this approach has not really

---

1. For a Bible-based concept of codependency, get my book *Escape from Codependent Christianity* through www.impactministries.com.

been that effective. After all, the world is not exactly running to the doors of the Church!

When a person is given a negative motivation for salvation, he begins the journey with God on a negative note. This usually sets the tone for his entire Christian experience. His Christian walk begins with a man-centered emphasis and not a God-centered Gospel. His faith now focuses on what he must do to earn God's approval instead of on what Jesus has already done because of God's great love for him. He strives to become lovable instead of accepting that God has done everything he needs for eternal life.

The word *gospel* means "good news"! Thus, if it is not good news, it cannot be the Gospel! The Bible says, "*Do you despise the riches of His goodness, forbearance, and longsuffering, not knowing that the goodness of God leads you to repentance?*" (Romans 2:4) The Church has had a tendency to underestimate the goodness of God. We have been convinced that our approach to reaching mankind is more effective than Jesus'. I think history proves we are wrong!

I've preached the Gospel around the world and seen masses of people come to Jesus. People are not swayed to repentance by a message of guilt and condemnation. Discovering the incredible love and value that God has for them is what draws people to salvation. When people start this journey from fear, they are robbed of the key elements for fulfilling their destiny. When people start this journey from God's love, their lives become an empowering adventure!

We have gone to the world and said, "God has no value for you unless you get saved." You might as well say we are inviting them into a relationship with a Father who rejects them. If the damage stopped there, we could recover them, but it doesn't. We then proceed to teach them,

"Unless you do everything God requires of you, He still has no value for you." With a message like this I'm surprised anyone has ever gotten saved. The Church is full of people who are struggling with low self-worth. As such, they become vulnerable to codependency, abuse of power, and manipulation.

My experience has been that those who get saved because of fear never become stable in their walk with God, unless they change their motivation. I have seen the tormented strugglers become stable and joyous as they moved from fear-based to love-based motivation. After all, if you're afraid of God, you can't trust Him. And trust (faith) is the basis of the entire relationship.

The Church should be a place of health and healing. It should be the place where people are safe to grow out of their past and come into a new future. It should be a place where people with problems are nurtured and helped. It should be a place of tolerance, love, and acceptance. It should be a place where love and fulfillment motivate growth and transformation, instead of a place where fear and rejection demand change. Thank God for the thousands of churches around the world that do provide a safe, positive environment. These are the ones that are reaching the world!

John 3:16 reads, *"For God so loved the world that he gave His only begotten Son...."* John used the Greek word *agapao* in this verse, which is translated as "love." The word *loved* means, "to hold dear, to cherish, to value." Kenneth Wuest defines it as, "to have value, to consider precious, to hold in esteem."[2] God doesn't look at man with hatred, contempt,

---

2.   Kenneth S. Wuest, *Word Studies in the Greek New Testament, Vol. III* (Grand Rapids, Michigan: Wm B. Eerdmans Publishing Company, 1968), p. 112.

or rejection. He holds man in esteem. He sees him as being worth the price that Jesus paid.

This is the message the world needs to hear. This is the message that each of us needs to receive! God loves us so much, He has so much value for us, and He considers us so precious that He has made every effort to ensure that we are eligible for all of His resources! Imagine how the rest of the world would respond if they knew how valuable they were to God. Picture what would happen if we reached the world with love instead of fear. Faith works by love.[3] We can only be filled with the fullness of God to the degree that we grasp His limitless love.[4] We only truly obey His commands when we walk in love.[5]

Man was created in an environment of love. God was his total source of physical and emotional fulfillment. He was created to derive his sense of personal worth from a source other than himself. Originally man looked to his relationship with God as his Father and Creator to derive his sense of worth and value. Man was created to gain worth from his relationship with a loving God.

*Our sense of worth and value
comes from our relationship with God.*

When man alienated himself from God, he began to look to other sources to find a sense of worth. Today, we

---

3. Galatians 5:6, KJV: *"For in Jesus Christ neither circumcision availeth any thing, nor uncircumcision; but faith which worketh by love."*
4. Ephesians 3:19: *"To know the love of Christ which passes knowledge; that you may be filled with all the fullness of God."*
5. Galatians 5:14-15: *"For all the law is fulfilled in one word, even in this: 'You shall love your neighbor as yourself.'"*

look to our jobs, our spouses, our talents, our athletic ability, and other things to make us feel right about ourselves. We look everywhere other than where we should—to our heavenly Father!

There are two basic reasons we do not look to God. The first reason is that our sin nature is a nature of fear. When Adam first became a sinner, he didn't immediately desire to do evil things. His first change was an emotional one—he suddenly became afraid of God.[6] Fear caused him to no longer trust God. This resulted in his pursuit of sin to meet his personal needs. He no longer trusted God as his provider. His negative sense of self robbed him of faith and confidence.

Having been born into sin, we have an inherent fear of God. Fear opposes love. As long as we hold to our fear of God, we cannot accept the love of God. To the degree that we accept the love of God, we will no longer be afraid of Him.

> There is no fear in love; but perfect love casts out fear, because fear involves torment. But he who fears has not been made perfect in love. We love Him because He first loved us (1 John 4:18-19).

Fear and love cannot coexist. We will experience either one or the other in our relationship with God.

The second reason men do not look to God for their sense of self-worth is that the message they have heard about God starts them off on a negative relationship with Him, just as we discussed earlier. Today, however, there is a new breed of church and pastor arising. There are now incredible

---

6. Genesis 3:10: *"So he said, 'I heard Your voice in the garden, and I was afraid because I was naked; and I hid myself.' "*

churches around the world that are investing in people in a way that points people to God as a loving and trustworthy source of life, love, and peace. They are establishing people in a relationship with a loving God. However, during the prior two thousand years, the predominant message of the Church has been one of wrath, fear, and judgment! The general public still sees God through the old paradigm of a judgmental religious world! Paul quoted the prophet Isaiah and identified this misrepresentation as the reason that the world hates God. *For 'the name of God is blasphemed among the Gentiles because of you' "* (Romans 2:24).

However, today millions of people around the world are coming to God because someone has told them about His incredible love. As such, they do not feel they are coming to a scrutinizing, faultfinding God from whom they need to hide their every flaw. This new breed of believer says, "I believe God loves me. I believe that He accepts me in Jesus." He derives his sense of worth from what he is worth to God—the life of Jesus!

You must know you have worth
before you can realize your dream.

It's essential that people recover their God-given sense of dignity and worth. It's imperative that we feel right about ourselves if we're going to realize our dreams and come into our full potential. And we must begin with the discovery of God's love. Then the transformation process is not propelled by the negative sense of God's disapproval. Instead, His love and acceptance make transformation a positive empowering experience.

My ministry experience has proven that people will only yield to the transformation process when they can do so without further damaging their personal sense of self-worth. Like Dave, many people have such a low self-worth that every hint that they could grow becomes a slanderous attack on who they are. They feel insulted by the suggestion that they should grow. A low self-worth is a trap that blinds them to the truth that could set them free.

You don't have to be caught in this trap. You can feel good about yourself as you make the journey of transformation. Through every step of the process, you can experience and be motivated by love and acceptance instead of wrath and rejection. Every new step you take forward in God will make you feel like a priest and king. It will draw you deeper into who you really are! *"To Him who loved us and washed us from our sins in His own blood, and has made us kings and priests to His God and Father, to Him be glory and dominion forever and ever. Amen"* (Revelation 1:5-6).

Work through these exercises to get to the heart of your relationship with God.

1. Did you get saved because of fear?
2. Have you since grown in the love of God?
3. Are you more motivated by the fear of God or by the love of God?
4. Are you changing because of the benefits it brings to you or because you think God does not accept you?
5. Find at least five scriptures that tell you that God accepts you now!

6. Make a list of the benefits that would come into your life by allowing personal growth and transformation to occur.

7. Prayerfully establish your intention to allow the skills, traits, and behaviors you desire to come into your life.

CHAPTER SIX

FROM THE BEGINNING

A part from God, it's impossible for any of us to establish a proper sense of self-worth. We are who we are, in relation to God. Once the God connection is abolished we sink to our lowest level of existence. The evolutionists and atheists in their quest to alienate God and exalt man have unwittingly robbed us of our only true source of dignity and worth. The world has not evolved into the manmade utopia that they claimed it would. In fact, quite the opposite effect has occurred.

Some historians believe that man's attempt to free himself from a connection with God came about as a reaction to the Church's control of science and the world. For many hundreds of years, the Church was the main source of oppression in the world. The Church ignorantly misinterpreted and misused Scripture as a means of controlling the thoughts and lives of the world. Governmental leaders used the Church's influence to control countries. The Church, by incorporating unscriptural ideologies, promoted a negative view of man, which left the unbeliever with only one reasonable option—abandon God!

It's easy to see how the Church's warped view of God would cause people to reject Him. The more appropriate thing would have been to establish a more biblical view of God. However, trying to understand God from the archaic, twisted doctrine of the Church would have been like coming into a very complicated thriller movie in the middle. It would be impossible to discern which character was the bad guy and which was the good guy. In order to understand God's relationship with man, we have to go back to the beginning. We must understand how God intended for man to live and function.

Mankind has always been plagued by questions about God's view and opinion. Historically, the Church has represented God as having a very negative view of man. Even scientists have considered man to be so insignificant that they've taught us we could not possibly be the only intelligent life in the universe. The Church, science, and even humanists have never even grasped a glimpse of God's highly favorable view of mankind. In fact, it's impossible to see the glory of man apart from the glory of God.

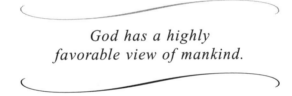

God has a highly
favorable view of mankind.

Psalm 8 begins like many psalms. It praises and acknowledges God. But this psalm unfolds a specific idea. The first verse acknowledges God as supreme Creator of all of heaven and earth: *"O Lord, our Lord, how excellent is Your name in all the earth, who have set Your glory above the heavens!"*

The psalmist of this passage then contemplates the question of all questions: *"When I consider Your heavens, the work of Your fingers, the moon and the stars, which You have ordained, what is man that You are mindful of him...?"* (Psalm

8:3-4) Many a person who has stood under the canopy of a beautiful, star-filled heaven and has pondered the great scope of creation has been overwhelmed with a feeling of gross insignificance.

As if creation itself is not enough to dwarf our sense of self, add the fact that a mighty God created all of it. The question remains to be asked, "If a Being great enough to create all of this exists, what could I possibly mean to Him?" How we answer this question strikes the core of our very existence. Answer it negatively and we spend our lives groveling at the feet of Almighty God, forever reminded of our insignificance. Life becomes filled with begging for undeserved favor and benevolence, and our faith becomes a millstone dragging us to the depths of despair, instead of the liberating freedom it is meant to be.

I believe the remaining verses of Psalm 8 were God's revelation to the psalmist. In these verses, the question is forever answered. Our sense of self-worth should be forever changed by these verses.

Consider verse 5: *"For You have made him a little lower than the angels."* The word translated as "angels" comes from the Hebrew word *Elohim*. This word is used to describe the Godhead.[1] This verse is not saying that man is a little lower than the angels; it is saying that man was created just a little lower than the Godhead. The angels weren't created in the likeness and image of God—man was![2] In fact, Hebrews 1:14 clearly explains that angels are sent to

---

1. Biblesoft's *New Exhaustive Strong's Numbers and Concordance with Expanded Greek-Hebrew Dictionary.* Copyright © 1994, Biblesoft and International Bible Translators, Inc.).

2. Genesis 1:26: *"Then God said, 'Let Us make man in Our image, according to Our likeness....'"*

serve us: *"Are they not all ministering spirits sent forth to minister for those who will inherit salvation?"*

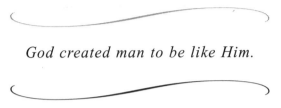

God created man to be like Him.

The last part of Psalm 8:5 is essential to understanding God's will for man's emotional makeup. *"And You have crowned him with glory and honor."* God did not create man to live a slave. He created man to live as royalty. As such, He crowned man with glory and honor—dignity and worth! *The Expositor's Bible Commentary* says, "The dignity of man is a gift from God."[3]

When a man is born of royalty, he also is royalty. Man was birthed from God Almighty. God breathed some of who He is into us. He imparted to us His very characteristics. He intended for us to be His family, His children, His heritage. We were so much like God that He gave us dominion over planet Earth. We were to rule and reign in His stead!

The psalmist completed his examination of man's significance to God and to all creation by stating, *"You have made him to have dominion over the works of Your hands; You have put all things under his feet"* (Psalm 8:6). We do not reign supreme over planet Earth by a random act of evolution or by accident or surprise. God gave us dominion. We may have misused it, but we received it because God established it. We have dominion!

---

3. Frank E. Gaebelein, *The Expositor's Bible Commentary, Vol. 5* (Grand Rapids, Michigan: Zondervan, 1991), p. 113.

Adam did not rule Earth by force. He ruled Earth with confidence. He had knowledge of who he was and he walked in it. There was no question in his mind that he was in charge. His ability to rule with certainty was the result of understanding his relationship to God.

We've all met people who feel completely right about themselves. They walk in as if they own the room. They have no need to impress. They seem oblivious to anything or anyone other than where their attention is focused. Everything seems to go right for these people.

Such are the lives of people who have a positive, healthy sense of self-worth. We mistakenly assume that they feel good about themselves because everything goes right for them. But the truth is, it's just the opposite! They have found their self-worth and from that flows their successes. The Bible affirms this: "*Your heart...affects everything you do*" (Proverbs 4:23, NLT).

On the other hand, people with no self-worth destine themselves for failure. Proverbs 17:20 says, "*He that hath a froward heart findeth no good*" (KJV). The word *froward* means "crooked." The heart is the seat of our sense of self. The person whose heart is not straight with God's Word, His view, and His opinion cannot find good. He is the person for whom things just don't seem to work out. His fate is doomed by the beliefs of his heart.

The beliefs of your heart
determine your view of your worth.

We all live and function at the level of our sense of self. How you view your worth is the product of the beliefs of your heart. God intended you to see yourself as His child, His heir, and as a ruler of the planet. He intended for your sense of dignity and worth to propel you through life with complete faith and confidence. It's crucial that you lay a foundation of dignity and worth to build upon in order to become the person you want to be. From a Bible-based, God-given sense of dignity and worth, all other aspects of fulfilling your destiny will emerge. Dignity and worth are the forces that will propel you into a life of destiny! And they are only found through discovering the reality of God's incredible love and value for you.

Complete the following questions and exercises to evaluate your current sense of worth.

1. How would you rate your personal sense of self-worth?

2. Take a few minutes and write out the feelings that you tend to have about yourself most often.

3. When you are faced with a new challenge, do you usually think you can or cannot succeed?

4. When meeting new people, do you expect to be accepted or put on trial?

5. When you see a photo of yourself, what is your first thought?

6. Do you feel like you are trying to win at life by coming from behind?

7. Write a brief paragraph detailing how you want to feel about yourself.

8. Affirm to God that you will begin to look to His value for you as your new source of self-worth.

CHAPTER SEVEN

CROSSING THE TIPPING POINT

The United States Army has a slogan: Be all that you can be! Everyone committed to becoming the person they really want to be is attempting to live that slogan. For so many people, however, the ability to live their potential seems to evade them. They do so many of the "right things." Their potential is obvious to others, but they somehow never seem to really "be all they can be."

Terri was one of those people. She was one of the brightest young women I had ever met. She had come to our church for quite some time. She was completing her last year of college. Her grade average was outstanding. When it came to passing academic tests, she pretty much "aced" the program. But in real life she never quite seemed to fulfill her potential. She fits into a category I call "potential people."

"Potential people" is my own term for those who have great potential but never seem to be able to fulfill it. I have seen so many "potential people" never really reach their life goals. Yet, based on their potential, they should be topping the lists in many areas. Potential, however, is never an indicator of what a person will really do with his life.

I learned the hard way that I should never depend on people based on their potential. Few things are as disappointing as being let down by someone you depended on because that person had such great potential. In fact, relying on someone based solely on his or her potential is an unsound approach to leadership. Scripture admonishes us to depend only on those who have proven themselves reliable. Not doing so can be a major cause of frustration and failure in leadership.

Potential is simply potential;
it does not guarantee its fulfillment.

Depending on a person's potential is not only frustrating for those who seek to lead them, it is even more disheartening for the ones who can't seem to live up to that potential. Their undeveloped capabilities become a source of frustration instead of a source of hope. They are condemned by what they should be able to do. Unfortunately, most of the people who influenced them allowed them to take shortcuts because they had so much potential, and they often never developed the discipline and work ethic necessary to bring their latent resources into actual productivity.

"Potential people" seem to have what some people refer to as a *tipping point* that they have never crossed. A tipping point is that point where the scales suddenly tip over in your favor and everything starts working for you. When I was a child, we would play on the seesaw. Invariably, because I was so skinny, I would always end up hanging in the air because I didn't weigh enough to bring the big kid on the other end of the seesaw back to the ground. He would usually sit there laughing at me while I struggled to shift the weight in my favor. That's when I would start scooting backward to find the tipping point. The tipping point was that place where the balance all starts to shift in my favor. You change the balance by changing your position. When I crossed the tipping point, I was able to shift someone much bigger than me up into the air—while I laughed.

Everyone knows some "potential people." These are the ones who may have done all the right things, but the balance never seems to shift in their favor. They have gone to school, they have studied, or they may simply abound with natural talent, but their talent never seems to really work for them.

I wanted to help Terri cross the tipping point in her own life. I wanted to see her turn her potential into something tangible. I had seen so many others cross the tipping point. I knew she could do it!

For some people, the tipping point comes with something they need to do. It comes with one methodology or application that they haven't yet tried. But once they take that step everything starts working for them. For most people, however, the tipping point is a change of beliefs. Those beliefs are usually an aspect of their self-perception that creates internal boundaries.

The writer of Proverbs says, "*Keep your heart with all diligence, for out of it spring the issues of life*" (Proverbs 4:23). The word *issues* could also be translated as "boundaries." The beliefs of our heart create the boundaries in our life. Until these limiting beliefs of the heart are changed, we will not cross our personal boundaries.

Potential is not a determining factor in crossing your tipping point! Having been born again, we are filled with all the wisdom, anointing, and power of God. Everything that God is comes into us to equip us to live our dreams and serve His Kingdom. If we could just find a way to simply be who we really are down inside, we would no doubt soar beyond our wildest dreams. The grace of God is in us, potentially empowering us to conquer every situation. But that potential must be realized or it becomes nothing more than the cause of frustration!

The beliefs in your heart
create the boundaries in your life.

The frustration of living with unfulfilled potential can be immense. It's like someone who starves to death even though he has money in the bank. The money was there, but he never spent it because he didn't know how to write a check! The power to save himself was at his fingertips, yet he still died.

So why would a person have the power to do something, yet not do it? If a person has the ability, wouldn't the results be automatic? Not necessarily. As the "potential person" has so painfully discovered, ability and success don't automatically go hand in hand! Having the power alone is not enough. It takes a catalyst to push the "potential person" into using his power to get beyond his boundaries.

Matthew 3:16 tells us when Jesus was endued with power from on high:

When He had been baptized, Jesus came up immediately from the water; and behold, the heavens were opened to Him, and He saw the Spirit of God descending like a dove and alighting upon Him.

Was the fact that Jesus received power a sufficient catalyst to launch Him into the fulfillment of His destiny? Or, was there something else?

Just before His ascension, Jesus promised His disciples, *"But you shall receive power when the Holy Spirit has come upon you; and you shall be witnesses..."* (Acts 1:8). They did receive the Holy Spirit, but did they all become powerful witnesses? Actually we have no record of many of the disciples ever doing anything significant. And those who did had their own personal struggles. It took Paul fourteen years to cross his personal tipping point to go forth with his ministry.

Regardless of your doctrine concerning the Holy Spirit, we can all agree that not everyone who has the Holy Spirit living inside them has become a powerful witness. Is there some factor we are missing? Is there something other than being endued with power that launches us forward in fulfilling our potential? Yes!

Approval is what turns
potential into personal power!

Verse 17 of Matthew 3 goes on to say, *"And suddenly a voice came from heaven, saying, 'This is My beloved Son, in whom I am well pleased.'"* The Holy Spirit coming upon Jesus gave Him potential power, but it was His Father's approval that gave Him the personal confidence to walk in that power. It was the power of approval that catapulted Him into fulfilling His potential! The sense of personal approval is something that few believers experience. For most people, it is their tipping point! It is the place where potential becomes true personal power!

Terri did not grow up in a home that was filled with approval and acceptance. In fact, her high performance did not emerge from a healthy sense of self. It was a desperate means to gain approval. Her parents, who probably meant well, used conditional acceptance as a means of motivation. When she achieved, she experienced acceptance and approval. When she did not live up to their expectations, though they were not unkind, they expressed their disapproval.

Few parents ever learn the art of expressing acceptance while disapproving of an action. Negative motivation as it turns out is not motivation at all! The result is conditional acceptance. In this kind of environment, no matter how good these children do, they feel like they should have done better. There is an abiding expectation of disapproval. Even when their works are approved, they don't feel approval as a person.

Consequently, many children are armed with a great education, and develop many incredible skills, but their sense of self keeps them from operating in those skills in a way that fulfills their potential. They begin to develop an image of their parents as impossible to ever please. Tragically, they will impose that image of their parents onto God.

Terri, like hundreds of others I have helped, worked a plan to alter her experience of God's approval. She started by establishing a new, more biblically based sense of self. Every day I had Terri do Heart Exercises from our Heart Physics® program,[1] during which she meditated on the reality that Christ was in her. As this became her reality, her entire sense of self changed. As time went by, she crossed her

---

1.   Heart Physics® is a biblical meditation program based on the teachings of the Lord Jesus. It is designed to help a person create a connection with God at the heart level. For more information, go to www.heartphysics.com.

personal tipping point and her education and other life experiences starting working for her instead of weighing her down. Like Jesus, she turned potential into real power.

Are you living more in your potential than you are in true success?

Here are some questions to evaluate where your tipping point is and some exercises to help you cross it.

1. Do you feel like you should have more success than you are currently experiencing?

2. Do you feel that you have the strengths to do what you want to do?

3. Do you feel you are limited and do not know why?

4. Make a list of areas where you know you have potential that has not been developed.

5. Does your present self-perception move you toward or away from your goals?

6. Affirm to God that you intend to develop a Bible-based sense of self-worth!

CHAPTER EIGHT

THE POWER OF APPROVAL

Approval is so incredibly empowering and so essential to healthy living. Young people crave it. They seem to want it from their parents more than anything else. No matter how old we are, we never seem to escape the search for approval. Conversely, the absence of approval is emotionally and physically devastating. We've all experienced it. When we're around someone who doesn't approve of us, someone we're sure will discover our faults, we can't even function normally. We seem to have two left hands. We fail at the easiest task. It is crippling!

Approval and disapproval tend to be magnifiers. The first will magnify positive tendencies and the second negative. Our every weakness grows in power in the face of disapproval. And our every strength gets stronger when it encounters positive, healthy approval. Until a person has established his self-worth through a meaningful, dynamic relationship with God, the approval and disapproval of others control his life.

I once heard this incredible statement, "The person who will influence your life the most is not the person you believe in; it is the person who believes in you."[1] This is so true. When someone believes in us, we feel safe. We settle

---

1. Source unknown

down and function at our best because we are not afraid of disapproval. Even failure has a different effect when there is an environment of approval. Failure becomes a necessary stepping-stone to learning and progress when there is no fear of rejection.

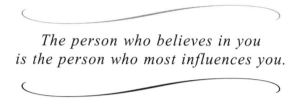

The person who believes in you
is the person who most influences you.

As a child I spent many summers with a favorite uncle. He was much stricter than anyone in the family. He expected the best all the time. When I stayed with him I had to work, and I had more responsibility. It was really quite challenging. But this man was one of the major positive influences in my life. Although he required so much, he had a unique ability to always make me feel good about myself. He always made me believe that I could live up to his standards. What could have been unrealistic goals beyond my reach became exciting challenges and learning experiences. He believed in me! With him, I experienced personal approval.

During the summer months I spent at home, I would get into all kinds of trouble. I would usually do things that were not only unacceptable, but also often illegal. When I was with my uncle, on the other hand, I never got into trouble. I didn't curse, I didn't smoke, and I didn't do any of the things that came so naturally for me in other environments. His high expectations and positive personal approval transformed my life for those few weeks every year.

This is the effect God's approval will have on us when we believe and experience it! This is the effect it had on Jesus.

Unlike our carnal concepts of approval, God's approval is not based on our performance; it is based on His value for us.

God said of Jesus, *"This is My beloved Son, in whom I am well pleased"* (Matthew 3:17). The phrase *well pleased* in the original Greek means, "to think well of." I can almost hear you shout, "Of course He thought well of Him; He was Jesus!" But like the psalmist discovered, God thinks well of us all. We are significant to God! "But why," you ask, "would God think so well of us if we are sinners?" Simple! He loves us with an undying, uncompromising, unfailing love—a quality of love that values the object of its affection; a love that holds us in high esteem; a love that considers us worthy of the price He paid for us. The Greek calls this kind of love *agape*. And this is how He felt about us even when we were sinners.

As Paul so eloquently stated:

> *But God demonstrates his own love us in this: While we were still sinners, Christ died for us. Since we have now been justified by his blood, how much more shall we be saved from God's wrath through him!* (Romans 5:8-9, NIV)

The apostle John indicated that the love of God is revealed in two key places. First John 4:9 says, *"In this the love of God was manifested toward us, that God has sent His only begotten Son into the world, that we might live through Him."* We can all grasp the fact that God loves Jesus. He was the *"only begotten Son"* of God. But consider this…although He loved Him, He loved us so much that He sent Jesus to pay the price for our sin. Jesus loved us so much He was willing to do it! Amazingly, He considered us worth the price! If He loved Jesus, yet required that He pay for our sins, then we each must ask the remaining question, "How much does He love me?"

Some of us think that God loves us but has no value for us unless we do everything right. We think that doing everything right is the source of His approval. But it's this natural reasoning that alienates us from the power of God's love and acceptance.[2] His Word says, *"But God demonstrates His own love toward us, in that while we were still sinners, Christ died for us"* (Romans 5:8). He didn't wait until we performed well enough. When we were at our worst, God still had value for us. Failure to believe this truth prevents us from experiencing His love and approval!

First John 4:10 goes on to say, *"In this is love, not that we loved God, but that He loved us and sent His Son to be the propitiation for our sins."* The word *propitiation* means, "the satisfying of wrath." Jesus became our sin, and God expressed all of His wrath for our sins on His Son Jesus. Jesus took all the punishments we deserved.[3] When He cried out, *"My God, why have You forsaken Me?"* (Matthew 27:46), He was not merely quoting scripture. He really was alienated from God. He was rejected so that we wouldn't have to fear that rejection. He experienced the disapproval so we wouldn't have to experience it.

Jesus, the One who was well pleasing to God, the One who had personal approval, went through what the English calls reconciliation. In the original Greek, the word for *"reconciliation"* literally means "an exchange." He did not simply buy us back to God; He bought us back by the process of exchange. God's wrath against sin had to be satisfied. Sin

---

2.   Romans 8:7: *"Because the carnal mind is enmity against God; for it is not subject to the law of God, nor indeed can be."*

3.   See Isaiah 53:4-5.

had to be paid for in the body of the sinner. That's why Jesus became our sin and took our punishment. That's part of why He had to become a man. Man brought sin into the world; therefore, man had to pay for sin.

But Jesus' work did not stop there. That still would have left us powerless before God. He became all that we were and suffered the consequences that we should have suffered. Through this exchange, God made it possible for us to become all that Jesus is—Priest, King, and Heir—and experience the benefits He deserved. It was a complete exchange.

If God's wrath is satisfied, if His approval for me is based in His value for me and not my performance, if Jesus was rejected so that I could be accepted, then I must realize that God approves of me—even when He does not approve of my behavior!

> *If Jesus was rejected so that you could be accepted, then you must realize that God approves of you.*

This is the place in our lives where we can overcome years of negative conditioning. We can leave the world of conditional acceptance behind. We can be empowered by this incredible love just as Jesus was when He walked the earth.

Imagine what it would do to your life if you could settle down and be at peace with God, having no fear of rejection. It would create an environment where failures are turned into learning experiences. It would allow you to function without fear!

Everything in us says, "This cannot be! This is too good to be true!" That's why it's called the Gospel—because it is great news! When the Bible talks about the carnal mind, it's talking about the natural mind, which reasons things out based on the natural process. Paul said the natural mind was opposed to the life of God. The natural mind alienates us from the law of life in Christ Jesus. It causes us to function in the flesh!

When Paul talked about the flesh, he was talking about the world of performance. The things you do in the flesh are basically those things you do to earn God's acceptance. You depend on your ability instead of on the work of the Holy Spirit. In the Old Testament, the people thought that keeping the Law would earn them the state of righteousness before God. They were in the flesh. The Law did not have the power to make anyone righteous. The Law was the most incredible self-help system in the world, but it was powerless to transform and empower!

The natural mind, the world of carnal reason, opposes all that Jesus accomplished. That is why we are told to renew our mind.[4] Most of us have spent our entire lives thinking and, subsequently, acting on the world's system of reasoning, which is based on performance and conditional love. That type of thinking prevents us from experiencing the abundant life for which Jesus paid such a high price.

In Romans 8:5 Paul told us, *"Those who live according to the flesh set their minds on the things of the flesh, but those who live according to the Spirit, the things of the Spirit."* There are people who refuse to give up the world's diabolical system of performance. Their minds are set on how well they can

---

4. See Romans 12:1-2.

perform. They feel accepted when they perform well, and they feel rejected when they do not. They falsely assume their own feelings to be confirmation of God's opinion of them as well. Their emotions affirm their self-deceit.

But there are other people who have their minds set on the work of the Spirit. These people trust in the work that the Spirit of God has done in them. They trust that God's Spirit has come into them and made them righteous and acceptable to God. The people who look to the finished work of Jesus are going to experience the peace of God and the quality of life that Jesus died to give us! Paul put it this way: *"To be carnally minded is death, but to be spiritually minded is life and peace"* (Romans 8:6).

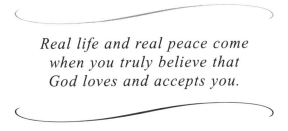

*Real life and real peace come
when you truly believe that
God loves and accepts you.*

Real life and real peace...this inward quality of life will invade your world when you understand and truly believe that God loves and accepts you. It will empower every aspect of your life. Your positive awareness and feeling of God's approval will become the emotional base from which you function. It's like starting every project with God Himself standing over your shoulder saying, "I believe in you. You can do this...and I'll help."

Once you are experiencing the power of approval, expect to win! Soon you will approach every task with a confidence that says, "I can't lose. Even if I don't finish the race first, I'll feel like I did." Nothing in your life will be the same when you believe and experience the power of God's approval!

Answer the following questions to determine if you are acting on the world's system of performance-based acceptance or living by God's unconditional acceptance.

1. Do you have a general feeling of approval or disapproval?

2. Do you feel that you will lose approval based on your performance?

3. Did you grow up in an environment of conditional approval?

4. Do you have a clear distinction between who you are and what you do?

5. Do you find yourself having difficulty in giving acceptance to others who fail?

6. Do you look to Jesus' finished work for your sense of approval before God, or do you look to your performance?

CHAPTER NINE

GOING BACK TO THE SOURCE

Genesis 1:26 clearly tells us that man was created in the likeness and image of God. This is a powerful statement. It means far more than having a mere resemblance to God. It means more than having similar attributes. When God created man, He breathed into him the breath of life. God breathed some of His own essence into man. That's right! Some of the substance of God came into man, and this essential component distinguished him from all of the rest of creation. He was now made internally of the same thing as God. All of this means that our spirit is forever a part of who God is!

We are connected to God in a way that exceeds anything we can understand. In Ephesians 5:30, Paul put it like this: *"We are members of His body, of His flesh, and of His bones."* The natural mind simply cannot grasp the way in which we are connected to God. Yet, even when that connection is not real and alive to us, it is forever alive to God.

Through scientific testing, modern physics has shown that when particles are separated by a great distance they are still somehow intrinsically connected. Although separated by physical distance, when a stimulus influences one particle, the other particle is simultaneously influenced. They are connected by a "string" that is unseen by the naked eye and has probably not yet been seen by any scientific equipment. But the test results undeniably confirm their relationship.

Based on what I call the principle of connection, man was totally connected to God. We were made of His essence. I believe Adam could feel and sense God. He felt totally connected to God emotionally, intellectually, and spiritually. Adam never felt the isolation and aloneness that people feel today. Never, that is, until he severed the connection.

Prior to this separation, however, Adam lived his destiny. He did so out of his sense of connection with God. He ruled his world. Everything that God did in planet Earth, He did through man, and there was complete harmony. God's will was done on earth as it was in heaven. God and man were connected in purpose and power!

Adam couldn't help but live his divine destiny. His sense of identity wouldn't allow anything else, just as your present sense of identity is determining your life. Living his destiny was not something he had to work up or confess into being. It was the plane of his reality based on his connection with God. He knew no other sense of existence.

We have lost this very sense of connection with God in modern Christianity. We know about God. We experience small glimpses of His eternal being. We have moments of peace that are quickly interrupted by our carnal existence on the "mindplane." This existence is all that the carnal mind can see. It is on this plane that our natural mind reasons.

But man cannot be who he is destined to be apart from his sense of connection to God. Nothing about man functions as it should; we do not live as long, our emotions are skewed, our perceptions are distorted, and our relationships are ineffective. But we manage to somehow make sense of it all in order to adapt to our disassociation with

God, and here we stay until we want to reestablish our connection to Him.

You see, one of the laws of God's Kingdom is that force is never acceptable. God never forces anyone to do anything. Neither does He force Himself onto anyone. Love cannot operate in the absence of free will. Therefore, in order for man to know the love of God, he must be given the freedom of choice. God never violates our choices.

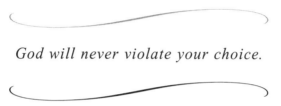

God will never violate your choice.

When Adam separated from God, it was not a mere problem of disobedience. We have imagined that God had a favorite fruit that He left in the garden and used it to test Adam's resolve. Because Adam disobeyed, God got mad and kicked him out of the garden. It was far more than that.

Adam's sin was not a mere act of disobedience. Adam chose to become the god of his own world.[1] James 1:14 tells us, *"But each one is tempted when he is drawn away by his own desires and enticed."* Adam could not have been tempted to be a god if that was not his desire.

He chose to separate himself from his relationship, as he knew it, with God. I'm sure he never realized the devastating consequences of being separated from God. He had probably come to believe that his self-worth was centered in himself instead of in God. Like his tempter and predecessor in rebellion, he reasoned his way into alienation from God.

---

1. Genesis 3:5: *"For God knows that in the day you eat of it your eyes will be opened, and you will be like God."*

After all, he was doing a great job of ruling planet Earth. He didn't really need God in every area of his life. Like many Christians, he most likely reasoned that he would be more than glad to invite God into any area when he thought he needed Him. But in the end, he would be his own god. And because God doesn't force Himself on anyone, He allowed Adam to make his choice.

Adam wasn't struggling with a simple issue of self-deception. In 1 Timothy 2:14, Paul explained, *"Adam was not deceived, but the woman being deceived, fell into transgression."* Adam's sin was of a completely different nature than Eve's. He sought a different goal altogether! Adam sought independence from God. And God allowed him to break that connection.

In Genesis 3:8-10, God came walking in the Garden to fellowship with Adam as He had always done. But this time Adam's response was different from before. He was afraid. Adam, in his newly chosen state of existence, experienced what he had never before experienced. Up until this time, he was so connected to God that he was not afraid of the power of God. That power was somehow a part of his very fabric. But now for the first time, he was afraid. He no longer experienced his life as one with God.

His fear was unexplainable to his own mind. Like all of us who "get caught," he started making random, nonsensical excuses. *"I was naked!"* What a lame excuse! I don't know if that was why he was really afraid. I think that may have been one of thousands of new reasons he had for being afraid of God. But at the core of it, there was one critical factor. He felt alone, separated, isolated from the one thing that gave him his sense of dignity and worth. He no longer felt the connection with God. He did not feel at one with his

Creator. He felt there was him and then there was God. Suddenly they were now two separate beings.

The Bible says, *"It is not good that man should be alone"* (Genesis 2:18). We are not made to be alone. And we are not made to be in relationships where there is a sense of, "us and them." "You and me" is not the prescription for a healthy life. There should only be "us." Eve wasn't created separately from Adam. She was not her own distinct being. She was part of Adam. She was taken from his fabric. There was to be the same connection between Adam and Eve as there was between God and Adam…oneness, connection, completeness! But when man lost his connection with God, the Creator of all things, on some level he also lost his connection with all things. He no longer ruled as he once did. Force became a carnal substitute for power. Adam's entire world changed both internally and externally.

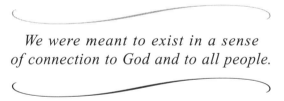

We were meant to exist in a sense of connection to God and to all people.

Man is meant to exist in a sense of connection to God and to all of mankind. Jesus said it like this: *"I and My Father are one"* (John 10:30). We tend to interpret that as some special relationship reserved for the Father and Jesus. But He showed us how men freed from the nature of sin should live. He modeled the restoration of man to God. He presented the idea of man being one with God and it was for this that they tried to kill Him.

Then the Jews took up stones again to stone Him. Jesus answered them, "Many good works I have shown you from My Father. For which of those works do you stone Me?" The Jews answered Him, saying, "For a good work we do not stone You, but for blasphemy, and because You, being a Man, make Yourself God." Jesus answered them, "Is it not written in your law, 'I said, "You are gods" '? If He called them gods, to whom the word of God came (and the Scripture cannot be broken), do you say of Him whom the Father sanctified and sent into the world, 'You are blaspheming,' because I said, 'I am the Son of God'?" (John 10:31-36)

The idea that any man could be one with God is more than our carnal, natural minds can process. It violates all of our natural logic.

More than anything, the idea of man being one with God, again, magnifies the isolation that most men feel. It threatens to take away life on the mindplane. And this life is what we know and trust! No matter how painful, we do not want to give it up!

When Jesus rose from the dead and poured out the Holy Spirit, the connection between God and man was restored for the first time since the fall. The Spirit in us should make us aware of God's presence in everything that we do. We should never again feel isolated or alone. That connection to God was what most people felt when they were first born again. Although too many people have lost touch with His presence, it can be restored. You can face every day with a confidence beyond what you have ever known just by making yourself aware of the living connection between you and God!

To maintain the awareness of God with us, we must practice His presence. Just as we can numb ourselves to the presence of our mate or children, likewise we can develop a lack of awareness for God's presence. We can grow insensitive to His touch and His voice. Relationships of all kinds must be nurtured to stay alive. We must take deliberate steps to maintain sensitivity to the people we love and to the God who lives inside us.

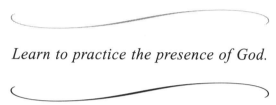

Learn to practice the presence of God.

God was Adam's Source, his life connection. There was a time in his life when he knew that connection. Most of us felt that connection when we were first born again because we made God our full and complete Source. Over time, we returned to old habits and replaced God as our Source. Church, prayer, the Bible, serving in ministry or any good thing can become our source. Instead of leading us to God, they can become activities that replace God. God has provided the connection to Him through Jesus. His presence and power, which is the Spirit of God, lives in us. We can reconnect to Him as our Source.

Here are some ways to begin reconnecting to God, your Source.

1. Acknowledge God as a part of your daily prayer life. If you don't know how to do this, order *The Prayer Organizer* from Impact Ministries by calling 256-536-9402 or by ordering from our website at www.impactminstries.com.

2. Make it a point to never face any day or any challenge without an awareness of God.

3. Acknowledge His presence by internally quoting scriptures.

4. The psalmist said to meditate on the Lord for stability. Ponder what it would be like for God to be present in every situation. Imagine the changes that it would bring if His power were present.

5. Acknowledge His presence and expect it to happen as you have seen it in your heart.

6. If Christ in you is not an abiding reality, use Heart Physics® to reestablish that connection.

CHAPTER TEN

THE CRUCIFIED REALITY

Barbara was a professional Christian counselor. After years of helping others, her own life was now falling apart. Her honesty was refreshing as she admitted, "I have great difficulty understanding the effectiveness you're experiencing in your counseling program."

"Well," I confessed, "it is all based on some incredibly simple factors."

"I know," she quickly fired back. "That's the problem. They seem too simple!"

Like millions of people, Barbara, a committed Christian, a trained counselor, and a passionate minister of the Gospel, had lost touch with the Gospel. She was stumbling over the basics of Christianity. It is so easy to forget that all of the complex tools we use in ministry should always bring people back to a few very simple realities. Sometimes we egotistically begin to think that the techniques we use are what really help people.

Techniques and methodologies are simply tools that counselors and ministers use. They are like roads that lead to a particular destination. The road, or method, we choose is determined by where the person is when they start the journey. But in the end, the road becomes insignificant—the destination is the only important factor.

The destination that I seek to help every person reach is a place of loving trust in the finished work of the Lord Jesus, a meaningful relationship with God the Father, and an abiding sense of "Christ in you!" This fulfills the part of my mission statement that says, "We exist to make people whole through the love of God...."

There is an old proverb that says, "If you think a book can help you, don't read the book. If you think a teacher can help you, don't seek a teacher." Books merely exist to lead us to our source. Teachers teach to lead us to our source. The moment we think *they* are the source we are deceived. Too often, the simple Gospel gets lost in the maze of methodology. The methods become more important than the Lord we seek to know. At that point, methodology becomes the stumbling block.

> *The message is more*
> *important than the methodology.*

As I began to talk to Barbara about the basics of the Gospel, she grew steadily more agitated. She insisted, "I know that! I know that!" Like too many people, she believed that information she could recall was the equivalent of knowing! In the New Testament, the word *know* is intrinsically linked to experiencing. Intellectual information is a far cry from an experienced reality.

When I asked her to describe her approach to counseling, she began to explain the need for every person to recall all of their past experiences and she explained a very elaborate and sometimes effective methodology for dealing with each past experience. I agreed that this technique is sometimes effective and occasionally essential. But I had a question!

I proceeded to inquire, "How do you explain the use of this methodology in light of this scripture?" I quoted Galatians 2:20, which reads:

> I have been crucified with Christ; it is no longer I who live, but Christ lives in me; and the life which I now live in the flesh I live by faith in the Son of God, who loved me and gave Himself for me.

After twenty minutes of talking in circles, it became painfully obvious that, like hundreds of others I have asked the same question of, she didn't believe the reality of this verse, nor did she incorporate this essential truth into her counseling ministry.

Becoming the person you want to be—the person who lives in consistent victory, prosperity, joy, and peace—is totally dependent on leaving the past behind. Jesus did not die and conquer death and hell to clean up your old life. He did all that to give you a new life. The person you used to be, not just what you used to do, is dead—you were crucified with Christ!

So the question begs to be answered, "If that old person is dead, why are you attempting to solve all of his problems?" If that person is not dead, then you did not actually get a new life in Christ and there is no such thing as the new birth. There is just the new effort!

In Christian counseling, it is sometimes crucial to deal with past issues; however, one does not seek to unravel the past. One seeks to accept the finished work of Jesus, to renew the mind in the resurrection realities, and to begin to experience God's empowering grace. You can't get on with your new life in Christ if you think there is anything left to resolve in the old life!

> *You can't get on with your new life in Christ if you think there is anything left to resolve in the old life!*

The heart of the Gospel is the fact that Christ gave Himself in a complete exchange. The New Testament word for this is *reconciliation*. The work done on the cross was more than a sacrifice. In this exchange, God *"made Him who knew no sin to be sin for us, that we might become the righteousness of God in Him"* (2 Corinthians 5:21). Jesus didn't simply carry our sin. He became our sin in order to free us from the power of sin and its effects.

God's justice required that the sinner pay for his own sin. Jesus became a man and lived a sinless life. He had no sin of His own to pay for. In Isaiah 53:6, the prophet describes what happened on the cross like this: *"All we like sheep have gone astray; we have turned, every one, to his own way; and the Lord has laid on Him the iniquity of us all."* We were the ones who went astray, yet all of our iniquity rushed upon Him. In the notable Old Testament commentary by Keil & Delitzsch, this is described as follows:

> Just as the blood of a murdered man comes upon the murderer, when the bloody deed committed comes back upon him in the form of blood-guiltiness inflicting vengeance; so does sin come upon, overtake (Ps. 40:13), or meet with the sinner. It went

forth from him as his own act; it returns with destructive effect, as a fact by which he is condemned. But in this case God does not suffer those who have sinned to be overtaken by the sin they have committed; but it falls upon His servant, the righteous One.[1]

The fact that Jesus literally became my sin is beyond my comprehension. But it should not be beyond my experience. The fact that He became my sin means that I do not live as a sinner saved by grace. The sinner is dead. He died on a cross two thousand years ago. Freedom from sin, and freedom from the power and consequences of it, is the essential truth for living the resurrected life in Christ now!

As Paul so eloquently stated, *"the life which I now live…I live by faith in the Son of God"* (Galatians 2:20). Jesus used His faith to obtain righteousness, to be raised from the dead, to give me a new life. The sinner I once was is now dead. The new me lives by the grace of God that comes to me through the faith in the Lord Jesus. The old me and all of my past issues died.

I remember what a relief it was to discover that I was not required nor did I need to go back into my past and find ways to overcome all the hurt, pain, rejection, and sin of that old man. He really is dead! I went to his funeral…it is called water baptism. That was the point where I accepted the death of the old and the resurrection of the new.

In the book of Romans, as Paul tried to help the church in Rome deal with this mystery, he gave the most simplistic

1.   C.F. Keil & F. Delitzsch, *Commentary on the Old Testament: New Updated Edition*, electronic version (Peabody, Massachusetts: Hendrickson Publishers, Inc., 1996).

advice: Reckon or consider yourself dead to sin (see Romans 6:11).

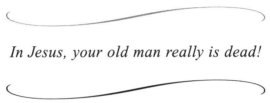

In Jesus, your old man really is dead!

This is what I shared with Barbara. At this point, Barbara acknowledged, "I know that's in the Bible, but don't you think that could be used as a form of denial?"

"It could only be denial if it weren't true!" I insisted. "This is true. We are dead to sin! But as long as we insist that we're not, we'll never experience this as our reality."

The Amplified Bible says it like this: *"Even so consider yourselves also dead to sin **and** your relation to it broken..."* (Romans 6:11, AMP). This is part of renewing your mind. You have to accept all of the New Testament realities as fact. You have to consider them so. The moment you consider them to be true, your perception changes; your basis of logic and reasoning changes. But more importantly, when you accept God's New Testament truth as real, you experience His grace that empowers you to live that reality.

Don't allow carnal logic to rob you of this cornerstone reality. If this is not the starting place for your new life, you will never escape the past. You will spend your life counseling it, cleaning it up, and trying to overcome it. That person is dead. Leave the dirt on the grave and move on! Accept the crucified reality...when Christ died, you died!

1. Have you been water baptized since you believed on the Lord Jesus?
2. Was that a place where you operated faith in the death of the old you and faith in the resurrection

of the new you through Christ's death, burial, and resurrection?

3. If you have been baptized, allow yourself to go back to that time in your memories. Then declare that you buried the old you. He is dead. You are now a new creation in Christ.

4. If you have not been water baptized, take the step and do it as an act of faith in this finished reality.

5. Every time an event from the past emerges to influence your thoughts or actions, stop and acknowledge, "That person is dead. I am not influenced by his life."

CHAPTER ELEVEN

STOLEN IDENTITY

There are two persons involved in your transformation process who have a significant influence on the outcome. One is a vision and the other is an illusion. One will encourage you and the other will become a stumbling block. The first person is your vision of who you want to be. The second person is who you think you are. The biggest deterrent in your becoming the person you want to be is the person you think you are.

We all have an illusion of ourselves that we have painstakingly created through time, tears, pain, and suffering. We have invested a lifetime into creating and supporting this illusion. We think we are the illusion!

Many of us seem to have great difficulty parting ways with this illusion. We work to keep it alive. It limits our experience in every dimension of life. It alienates us from God's life and power, which can free us from our past with all of its limitations.

Two thousand years ago our old man—all that we were apart from God—was crucified. That death is not something we need to make happen. It is the reality. When we receive Jesus, we accept the death of our old man. In fact, water baptism is designed to be the place where we specifically exercise faith in that death and acknowledge the resurrection life that we are now empowered to live. Water baptism is a ceremony designed to compel us into the reality of resurrection life!

Like the death of any loved one, all that we have left of our old man to hold onto is the memory. People commonly hold the memories of a loved one as long as they can. This is one of the major reasons why we don't pass through the grieving process in a timely manner. We reason that if we let go of those memories we will lose the person. Such is the case with our old man. We think that if we let go of the memories of the old man, we will lose our identity...and that is true. However, it's that identity that limits our lives with God. No one can be two people at once. You can't be who you want to be if you think you are who you used to be!

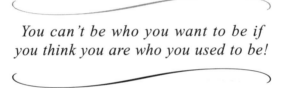

You can't be who you want to be if
you think you are who you used to be!

Your old identity is established by the sum total of your life's experiences. Everything that has ever occurred in your life and all of the judgments you have passed about those events shape and define who you believe you are. But this identity is only an illusion. This is because all of your memories are really only distortions of reality. The things you experienced did not happen as you remember them. You simply remember how they affected you.

Some studies indicate that every time you remember something and you have new feelings and experiences, you will alter that memory. The next time you think of it, it will be altered by how it affected you the last time you remembered it. Thus, the false reality grows.

So what if you do remember it correctly? Reliving a past event has never solved a problem. It usually only muddies the waters, complicates the issue, and reinforces the illusion of how real it is. Even more destructive, it reinforces the idea that those past events continue to destroy your life today. This is only a partial truth. If those past events are destroying your life today, it's because you are breathing life into them. We all have a penchant to do this.

We pretend past events still have the power to hurt us. We pretend like they can bring us pain. I'm sure you would insist, "I'm not pretending. This really does cause me great pain." Don't misunderstand me! The pain is real. But acting as if that old person is still alive is what you are pretending.

Our attempt to hold onto our old identity keeps us locked into the old life with all of its problems. We don't need to crucify the old man. He has been crucified already. We simply need to accept his death and let his memory die. That will only happen as we assume a new identity, a new sense of self, based totally on the finished work of Jesus. But many of us choose not to do this. Even though we have received a new life from Christ, we instead choose to steal back the identity of the old life.

> *Holding onto your old identity*
> *will lock you into your old*
> *life and all of its problems.*

Stolen identity is a real problem in the electronic world. People can get information about you and begin to live your life and spend your money. Others go to the graveyard and find the grave of someone close to their age. They obtain that person's birth record, then use it to get a social security card and a driver's license. Some identity theft experts even learn about the person they are imitating. They set out to live the dead person's life.

Likewise, you have stolen an identity. You have done your research. You have learned everything you can about someone who has died. You have memorized his every experience and his every pain, and you are pretending that it is you. You have so effectively convinced yourself that it really is you that you feel his pain. You weep when you think of his memories. But those are not really your memories. They are the memories of a dead person. But you have so identified with those memories that you have come to believe they are yours.

Some cutting-edge research indicates that our heart, not our intellect, gives us our long-term memories. Our long-term memories combine to establish our identity. But, when we accept Jesus, we are supposed to believe in our heart that God raised Him from the dead. As we renew our mind, we are to believe in our heart that Christ lives in us. And this serves to change the experience of our heart.

One of the ways you know you believe something at the heart level, as opposed to the intellectual level, is when this belief alters your sense of identity. Until your belief in New Testament truth changes the way you see yourself, it is more of an intellectual concept than a heart belief! Until it is a heart belief, it will not change your life.

When I believe in the resurrection of the Lord Jesus from His crucified death and finished work of salvation, in my heart, it does something to my sense of self. As I believe on Christ in me, I not only see myself differently, but I also experience myself as a different person. The person I used to be becomes more like the memory of someone I knew very well. But that person wasn't really me! In fact, I don't really care much for that person today. I'm actually glad he's gone!

We can't get on with resurrection life if all of our focus is on our former life. That life was a shame. Let it die the death it deserves. Sometimes after we lose someone, we re-shape our memory of him. We block the bad and only remember the good. I have heard women talk about their husbands as if they were loving saints when in reality they were violent abusers. We do the same thing with our past identity. That person was taking us to hell. They may have had a few admirable qualities in some limited areas, but that life was death.

If we heed the admonition to renew our minds, we will begin to put on the new identity we have in Jesus. We will discover all that we are in God and start to see ourselves in this new light. As we renew our minds, this new identity becomes our sense of self. To the degree that this becomes our reality, we will live in this new identity.

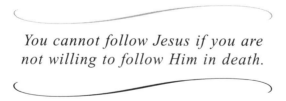

You cannot follow Jesus if you are not willing to follow Him in death.

Jesus tried to explain His upcoming death to His disciples. Although He dreaded the pain and shame of death, He knew death was the only way to discover the ultimate measure of the Father's glory. This concept was beyond the grasp of Peter's natural mind. He actually rebuked Jesus.

He was sure this was no way to establish a kingdom. But Jesus responded to him by saying:

> *For whoever desires to save his life will lose it, but whoever loses his life for My sake will find it. For what profit is it to a man if he gains the whole world, and loses his own soul? Or what will a man give in exchange for his soul?* (Matthew 16:25-26)

There is no way to follow Jesus if we are not willing to follow Him in death. We don't have to suffer death for our sins; Jesus paid that price. He died the death that awaits every person born into sin. The question is, will we accept that death? Will we lay down all that life with all of its memories and its false identity? And will we now see ourselves as God has made us to be through Christ? To hold onto the illusion is a vain attempt to save your life. You are already dead. To accept that death is the way to live in a new power, a new strength, and a new destiny!

1. Based on your memories, accomplishments, and failures, write one page telling who you are.

2. Take that list to a safe place and burn it. As it burns, verbally declare, "This is the death I deserved. This person is dead."

3. Make a new list of all the strengths, benefits, and privileges that God's Word says are yours through the resurrection of Jesus.

4. Make a list of how you now choose to live your life with limitless power and unlimited resources.

5. Review this list daily until it is how you see your future differently.

6. Always acknowledge God as your Source for liv-
    ing the life you have chosen.

CHAPTER TWELVE

CREATING A FALSE REALITY

There is a biblical principle that says what you give your attention to grows in your mind. When we focus on God as the object of our worship, our experience with Him grows. The reality of His presence abounds to the degree that we think about, talk about, and focus our attention on Him. The psalmist said, "*Oh, magnify the Lord with me*" (Psalm 34:3). In essence he was saying, "Let's make God bigger in our experience."

You can't actually make God bigger or more powerful, but you can magnify your experience of His power. You can experience more of who He is by focusing more of your attention on Him. In Psalm 34:1-2, the psalmist explained how he does this work of magnification: "*I will bless the Lord at all times; His praise shall continually be in my mouth. My soul shall make its boast in the Lord.*" His continual talking and thinking about God made Him bigger and more powerful in his personal experience until it altered his sense of reality.

All of us live in the reality that we create in our minds. But God has a reality that He calls us to participate in. In His reality, we are all free from sin; we maintain absolute victory over sickness; we live in peace and prosperity. In order, however, to enter His reality, we must give up our own.

Our reality, to the degree that it is inconsistent with His, is an illusion. Our reality, however, is the only life we know. It is based on years of experience. We have mountains of evidence that says, "This is real." When we accepted Jesus as Lord, that old man died, but we may unintentionally have kept the reality of that former life alive in our minds simply because we didn't understand or accept that we now had a new life.

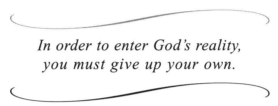

*In order to enter God's reality,
you must give up your own.*

On receiving Jesus, we were given a new heart and a new spirit. For a brief period of time, as new believers, we experienced a powerful new sense of self. Since we were not taught to renew our minds, we tended to look to the only resource we had for interpreting and understanding life...our past! This looking to the past resulted in corrupting our heart. It alienated us from the life of God that was in us through knowing the Lord Jesus Christ (see Ephesians 4:18).

Paul said, *"And those who are Christ's have crucified the flesh with its passions and desires"* (Galatians 5:24). The flesh is the ability, the strength, and the deeds—whether good or bad—of the old man. The New Testament calls us to "die to self." This is not an invitation to asceticism, self-hatred, or personal denial. This is a call to accept the death of the old man. And it is equally a call to put on the new man. You can't crucify your old man. You can't make him any more dead than he is. All you can do is *consider it so* in Christ. When you accept the death of the old man, all of his passions die with him. You free yourself from the past!

Barbara, the Christian counselor from Chapter Ten, had built her life and counseling protocol on her testimony, or at least what started out as a testimony. A testimony is usually an account of victory. For too many Christians their testimony is simply their account of the past. Their past experiences become the standard for measuring and judging reality. Instead of establishing a life paradigm from the Bible and using that as a basis for interpreting and understanding life, they use their experience as a means to understand and interpret God's Word.

Just as surely as we can make our experience with God greater in our sense of reality, we can create a false reality. We can empower an imagination to the degree that it controls our life. Anything we ponder long enough becomes real in our experience. Instead of salvation being the place where we finally let the past die, far too many of us are led to believe that salvation gives us the tools to fix the past. Then we spend our entire Christian life "messing around" with something that is over.

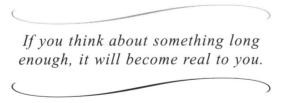

If you think about something long enough, it will become real to you.

Barbara's own experience with her past was one that never ended. She never got over the past. In some ways it seemed positive, even honorable. It seemed that she was fully committed to self-improvement. But the truth is that she kept her past alive. She accepted a lie over the truth. Her life was being squandered on an illusion.

Everything we do to solve the problems of our past life keeps that life alive in our experience. And if we involve ourselves with the past long enough, the illusion becomes our reality! Instead of coming into a new identity in Christ, we become more deeply submerged into our old identity with all of its problems.

Barbara continued to work with and deal with her past. She thought it seemed ridiculous to just consider it dead! Her experience justified her opinion. But her experience was fueled by a wrong focus—a focus that created a false reality! When experience and the Word of God do not agree, we must choose which reality we will make our own.

If my old man is dead, he has no influence over my present life—unless I create the illusion that it really was me who suffered all the shame and pain of the past. When I was eighteen years old, I went home to visit my mother. While I was there, my stepfather tried to kill me in my sleep. I still bear the gaping scars in my body. Years later, just before his death, I led my stepfather to the Lord. I had a deep passion for him. Someone once asked me if I had difficulty forgiving him for all he had done to me. As I thought about the question, the answer was, "He did all that to someone else." The hurts he inflicted then had no power over my current actions. The person who suffered those wrongs was dead.

"You don't know what's happened to me" is the battle cry of the person who seeks to live in the illusion of the old self! I realize people have experienced things that are beyond my ability to imagine. And while I have deep empathy for their suffering, I cannot let their experience change the Word of God. Your old man is dead and the old identity with it. Put him off so you can *put on the new man which was created according to God, in true righteousness and holiness*" (Ephesians 4:24). The problem is you think that the old person is really you. This is not true. You are a brand new creation.

It is impossible to put on a new identity while holding onto the old. The identity that you magnify in your thoughts, the "you" that you think about, becomes your sense of reality. And you become empowered by that sense of reality. The old you is dead! To think about yourself as that person is an illusion, a false reality. Yet, you can imitate that person. You can remember how he handled life's problems and imitate his ways. Or, you can think about the identity of the new you.

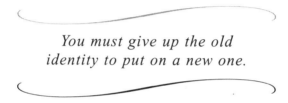

*You must give up the old
identity to put on a new one.*

Paul told the Ephesians to *"put on"* this new man. He didn't say, "Fix the old man." Putting on the new man is the process of renewing your mind, bringing yourself to a place where you see who you are in Christ. There is no nobler task, there is no more crucial step, than putting on the new you. But it is a way of life that you must choose. It is the laboring to enter into rest. It is the end of the power of your past.

Some of you are deceived into thinking that your struggle with sin is proof that you are still the same old person. Your sins, however, do not prove that you are the same person. They prove that you think you're the same person. They prove that you have failed to enter into the rest that comes with your new identity.

In the Old Testament, God prepared a place of rest for the children of Israel. It was called Canaan. The generation that received the promise didn't believe they could actually enter this place of rest. Consequently, they spent their lives roaming in the wilderness. The wilderness experience is the only alternative for the person who will not enter into the place of rest that God has prepared.

Our place of rest is not a geographic location. It is a state of being. Our place of rest is in Christ. This is the realm where we receive a new life based on the promises of God and a new identity based on the finished work of Jesus! Using the analogy of the children of Israel, the writer of Hebrews said:

> *For this Good News—that God has prepared a place of rest—has been announced to us just as it was to them. But it did them no good because they didn't believe what God told them. For only we who believe can enter his place of rest* (Hebrews 4:2-3, NLT).

Your toiling with problems is not proof that the old you is still alive. It is proof that you do not believe there is a new you. The old you was subject to the law of sin and death. Jesus died so you could be free from sin and its power.

> *For we know that our old self was crucified with him so that the body of sin might be done away with, that we should no longer be slaves to sin—because anyone who has died has been freed from sin* (Romans 6:6-7, NIV).

As long as you hold to the illusion that you are that old person, you will never escape the sins of the past. Every counseling session that takes you to the past reinforces the false reality. Every time you use an experience from your past to justify your present choices and actions, you deny the finished work of Jesus, you magnify a vain imagination, and you empower an illusion that takes control of your life.

Ask yourself these questions to determine which reality you are living.

1. Have you accepted the death of the old you?
2. Do you find yourself using your past as a justification for your actions?
3. From this moment forward, every time you catch yourself thinking about the past life, remind yourself, "That person is dead. I am a new creation."

Chapter Thirteen

Altered States of Reality

When I was a young man, I threw my lot in with the 60s revolution. If you weren't a part of that era, it's hard to imagine the issues that drove the unrest. My generation discovered that our government was less than forthright. My friends and classmates were giving their lives in Vietnam, a war that seemed politically and economically motivated. We weren't allowed to take our black friends to the same restaurants we frequented. Social injustice abounded and our voices were not being heard. We were angry, frustrated, and disillusioned. The truth demanded that we take action, but the cause was larger than we could cope with. Life seemed hopeless.

Hopelessness always produces a need to escape. To escape the world we couldn't face or change, we sought to exist in an altered state. We used drugs as a way to avoid issues that were beyond our control. That altered sense of reality made us feel that everything was all right even though it was getting worse by the minute. Getting high seemed better than suicide, but it wasn't much of a quality of life! I didn't find my ultimate escape from the futility of existence until the old me died at the foot of the cross. The change in me was dramatic. I suddenly had a new life, and along with that new life came a new sense of hope.

As a new believer, I was naively surprised to discover how few Christians seemed to live in any great degree of victory. As I talked with believers about life, about their dreams, and sometimes about their struggles, I found that few actually embraced the teachings of Jesus in a literal way. I was shocked by the lack of conviction. I was appalled by the apathy.

It was as if the Pied Piper had danced through town and played them a hypnotic lullaby that swept them into a trance and altered their sense of reality. "Yes, Jesus is Lord, but most of what He taught no longer applies," seemed to be what everyone believed but what no one actually said! What kind of sense is that? I couldn't comprehend their attitudes that said, "I will trust You with my eternal destiny, but not with my life." The absence of coherent logic in that was bewildering.

As I discussed this with my pastor, he explained, "Son, the Bible is the only book in the world that fully intelligent people can open and instantly lose their minds!" It took me years to understand the down-home wisdom in his statement. They *were* in a trance. The "piper" was the unbelieving church and the "melody" was religion! I once heard the late John Osteen say, "Religion is like a vaccination. It gives you just enough of the real thing so you can't actually catch it!"

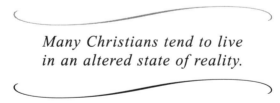

Many Christians tend to live in an altered state of reality.

Many Christians tend to live in an altered state of reality. They know they are not sinners. But they are not fully convinced they are heirs of God. They know God made promises. They are not certain, however, that they qualify for the promises. They are aware of the teachings of Jesus, but there is mass uncertainty about which ones really apply to them. They have enough faith to believe they will go to heaven when they die, but they are not sure they can abide in the Kingdom of God while they are alive. They know Jesus was crucified, but they are unclear about what that means for them!

Like the children of the 60s, they choose to live in an altered state of reality rather than face what they do not understand. They are afraid to choose God's reality; therefore, they choose something less challenging and more reasonable to the natural mind. They create a reality that contains enough truth to provide relief, but not enough power to give victory. It is like a stupor that numbs the pain but limits life.

The Bible consistently warns against living in an altered state. The King James Version usually uses the term *drunkenness* for this state. Our culture dictates that we translate "drunkenness" as a mere issue of alcohol. But it has far greater implications than just alcohol.

The problem with alcohol is that too much of it produces an altered state of consciousness. When a person is drunk, his perception changes; he is not alert or aware. He often develops a skewed sense of reality! He becomes vulnerable to all kinds of attacks. His imagination becomes distorted, yet all the more vivid.

In the 1960s, young people on drugs jumped from rooftops and windows, plunging to their deaths because they thought they could fly. The destruction of a substance-induced altered state was characterized through such bizarre behavior. However, there are other altered states that are as equally damaging as drunkenness. Luke 21:34 warns:

> *But take heed to yourselves, lest your hearts be weighed down with carousing, drunkenness, and cares of this life, and that Day come on you unexpectedly.*

Anything that affects your heart creates an altered state of consciousness. We are repeatedly warned throughout the New Testament to remain sober minded. While we may have developed a life of abstinence in the most obvious areas, we still engorge ourselves on vain imaginations, which are the ultimate "drunkenness" for the believer.

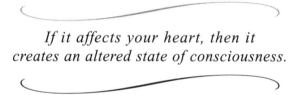

If it affects your heart, then it creates an altered state of consciousness.

Vain imaginations are thoughts, ideas, or opinions that stand in opposition to God's Word. In the passage from Luke, Jesus was describing something that the original language likens to a seizure or a sudden onset of pain. Altered states cause you to head down paths of destruction that don't seem too dangerous. But when disaster strikes, it comes like a seizure, suddenly and unexpectedly. You have no control once you begin to go over the edge.

The intoxicated driver doesn't realize he is weaving across the line until it is too late. The person who overdoses has no idea that he is minutes away from having his heart explode. The drunk doesn't realize how loud he is talking until he is asked to leave. Deception is the common denominator in all of these examples. Each person thinks he is in total control until it is too late! This is also the plight of the believer who lives in an altered reality that denies his union with the death, burial, and resurrection of Jesus!

Paul and Peter both gave repeated warnings to be sober minded and alert. A sober person sees things as they really are. Jesus, John, and Paul admonished us to turn from darkness and walk in the light! As a believer, I must open my eyes to truth and refuse to live in dark uncertainty concerning the finished work of Jesus! I must choose to live in the reality of God's Word even though my intellect may not be able to grasp it entirely. To be clear-minded, I must answer the questions, "Am I a new creation or not? Is the old me really passed away? Am I freed from sin's power and consequences? Was my old man really crucified with Christ, or is that just a religious platitude?"

Until I am willing to wholeheartedly embrace the teachings of Jesus, I am in darkness. I may not be in total darkness; however, it's not bright enough for me to see my way clearly. My struggle with the past ends with the acceptance of the death of the old man. When I consider it so, the old man loses his grip of my life.

However, giving up the old man does introduce one of the most threatening scenarios I have ever considered. If I give up the old man as my source of identity, I also give up all of my excuses. The way people treated me, the trauma of my childhood, and the injustices suffered in my past all fade into memories that belong to a different person. Though I remember that person, I don't own that identity anymore.

When I leave my altered sense of reality, then and only then does the promise of living as a new creation begin to look like an attainable reality. As I let go of the old identity, the light of a new identity begins to emerge in my heart, and I begin to see myself in Christ instead of in the flesh. In 2 Peter 1:19, the apostle said it so eloquently:

> *And so we have the prophetic word confirmed, which you do well to heed as a light that shines in a dark place, until the day dawns and the morning star rises in your hearts.*

In Paul's writing, he taught us how to lay hold of reality. Like Peter and the other New Testament teachers, he identified the mind as the place where our warfare is fought. We struggle when our own views and opinions rise up to oppose God's reality. We seek to create a Gospel that fits our corrupt logic, limited faith, and finite understanding. In 2 Corinthians 10:4-5, Paul called this vain imagination a stronghold. *"For the weapons of our warfare are not carnal but mighty in God for pulling down strongholds, casting down arguments...."*

*We struggle when our own views
and opinions oppose God's reality.*

The word *argument* (or *imaginations,* as the King James translates it) comes from the Greek word *logos.* Strong's explains this as an inventory.[1] We create a logic based on our inventory or assessment of the situation. In the altered state, we somehow fail to realize that our logic denies the logic of God and stands opposed to the finished work of Jesus.

---

1. Biblesoft's *New Exhaustive Strong's Numbers and Concordance with Expanded Greek-Hebrew Dictionary.* Copyright © 1994, 2003 Biblesoft, Inc. and International Bible Translators, Inc.

Paul went on to explain how to cast down our carnal logic:

> ...casting down arguments and every high thing that exalts itself against the knowledge of God, bringing every thought into captivity to the obedience of Christ (2 Corinthians 10:5).

We must interpret everything in light of Jesus' obedience to death, burial, and resurrection. If our logic denies His obedience and finished work, then it must be cast down!

Our arguments, reasoning, and logic do not simply present a debate between our opinion and God's; they oppose the knowledge of God. The word *knowledge* comes from the Greek word *gnosis*. This is a knowledge that is based on experience. We can't experience Christ's finished work if we embrace a logic that denies it! Thus, our diminished life experience becomes a false validation that our opinion is in fact correct. We live a lie that supports the lie; but even worse, it limits our experience of God!

Just recently I talked with a lady whom I had known for years. She explained her struggle against the truth. She said, "This was just so good that it seemed too far out." Ironically, during the times in her life when she embraced God's truth, she lived in victory. During the times when she drew back from her acceptance of God's truth, her life was in what she described as a limbo or fog. As bad as her altered sense of reality was, it was at least something she could understand. But when she chose to believe the truth, she began to understand and experience the truth!

We must choose to come out of the darkness. We must choose to accept a reality that is far above our logic. Only a conscious choice to accept God's reality above our own altered reality will shatter the illusions in which many of us are trapped. Only a life lived in conscious acceptance of God's reality produces hope!

Take a moment now to answer these questions, then begin to change your reality!

1. Are you committed without reservation to everything the New Testament teaches?

2. Are you aware of any opinions you hold that are inconsistent with the New Testament reality?

3. Will you accept God's reality above your own experience?

4. Do you look to your past as a way to justify or explain present behavior?

5. Make it a practice to no longer use your past as an explanation.

6. When you mishandle something, apologize, make it right, and offer no explanation.

7. When excuses emerge, refuse to identify with them. Remind yourself that the person with those excuses is dead.

CHAPTER FOURTEEN

THE HIDDEN MAN OF THE HEART

Many components are needed to do what you want to do with your life. We all need to develop new skills to keep us in pace with a world that is rapidly changing. Education and training is always to our advantage. We could all occasionally benefit from a little advice or counseling. All of these are factors that, when used properly, can help us in the functional aspect of life. But they are mere tools. They have nothing to do with who you are. Tools cannot help you to *become*; they can only help you *do*! They are not the source of your identity. You—the real you—determine how you will use these tools.

Every day millions of people the world over acquire a good education. Some complete counseling programs. Still others experience major life breakthroughs. None of these things guarantees their success, however. In fact, after making considerable advancements, some people still fail at life. They had hoped the tools would be adequate substitutes for dignity and worth. But there are no substitutes!

The moment we place the hope of "being" in any external arena, we enter the delusion of the mindplane. We vainly attempt to dress the outer man and clean him up...the one that has been crucified with Christ...the one that is dead. This is little more than adding imagination to illusion. Nothing really changes other than in our thoughts.

Most of our life's efforts to become who we want to be are like putting makeup on a dead man. You can make him look good, but you can't bring him back to life. The old you is dead. You can't make him die, and you can't bring him back. You can only accept or deny the reality. Refusal to accept this reality causes you to become a shadow boxer—a person who struggles with imaginary issues!

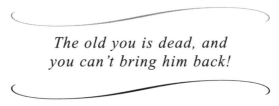

The old you is dead, and
you can't bring him back!

Since your struggle with your old self is an illusion, it never ends. You cannot end a battle that only exists in your mind. You can only change your mind! This illusory you sucks the life out of every moment and every hope. It steals your attention away from who you really are in Christ and draws it back to the illusion. All the while, it promises that it will one day bring you into the reality of who you hope to be. This illusion that claims to offer you a future victory is what keeps you from being the person you want to be. It alienates you from the reality of your new identity!

No matter how much you clean up that illusion, no matter what you do to improve that sense of identity, it is still false. Any attachment to that identity alienates you from the Spirit of God, thus alienating you from the grace of God. Grace is God's power that works in you and enables you to do and be all that God says you can do and be. God can't give grace to your vain imaginations. He has no salvation for the you that is already dead!

Paul said we should *consider* ourselves dead to sin. Why? Because sin only has power over a man as long as he is alive. When you die, sin loses its power. *"Even so consider yourselves to be dead to sin, but alive to God in Christ Jesus"* (Romans 6:11, NASB). Faith looks at the outrageous claims of God's Word and considers them to be so! Faith does not try to make them happen. Trying to make them happen gives testimony to the fact that you do not believe they have already happened. You can't make Jesus be crucified. He was crucified. You can't make Jesus rise from the dead. He has risen. You can't make Him Lord; He is Lord! And you can't make yourself free from the limitations of your past existence. You are free. All of these things are the glory of God. All we can do is consider them so. Faith accepts God's view and opinion as a present reality. When God's opinion becomes our opinion, His reality will become ours. Then we will experience life in Christ as it really is.

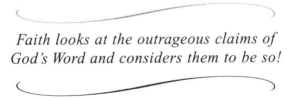

Faith looks at the outrageous claims of God's Word and considers them to be so!

The Greek word *doxa* means "glory." The glory of God is beyond description. But there is one final concept to the glory of God. All of His splendor, all of His greatness, all of His majesty exists because it is God's view and opinion of reality. It is His choice! God's Word, which is His opinion, creates a glorious reality called the Kingdom of God.[1] The Kingdom of God exists on a plane that is accessible to all

---

1. The Kingdom of God is not heaven. It is the realm wherein God's realities work. One can be saved but not be living in the Kingdom of God.

men. But it can only be entered internally. You know that you are still living on the mindplane when your life doesn't change. When you are living in the Kingdom of God, your life will change.

There is no possible way to connect to the Kingdom through any external source. It can't be found in any outward place or form. This was a common misconception of the Pharisees.

> *Once, having been asked by the Pharisees when the kingdom of God would come, Jesus replied, "The kingdom of God does not come with your careful observation, nor will people say, 'Here it is,' or 'There it is,' because the kingdom of God is within you'"* (Luke 17:20-21, NIV).

In this passage, the root word for "when" means "where." The Pharisees could have been asking, "When and where will the Kingdom come?" Jesus' answer seems to place the emphasis on "where." The where is the heart! It is only when we accept, focus on, and live from the internal realities of the Kingdom of God that we actually experience His power.

The new you can settle for the reality of the mindplane. However, that choice will become the reality that governs your life. In so doing, you limit yourself to the laws of that plane, which are in total opposition to God's realities. Thus you will see in your life the fulfillment of Romans 8:7: *"...the carnal mind is enmity against God; for it is not subject to the law of God, nor indeed can be."*

In Romans 8:5, Paul explained that the problem lies in the fact that the natural mind is focused on the flesh. The focus of the mind determines the reality we experience. If my mind is focused on the natural, intellectual plane—the mindplane—then my reality will be there, and I will live in an illusion of my past life. My intellectual beliefs cannot produce the abundant life promised by Jesus. If my mind is focused on the spiritual truths in God's Word, then my reality will be based in the Kingdom of God. I can only experience real life when I believe God's Word in my heart as a present-tense reality!

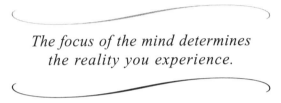

The focus of the mind determines the reality you experience.

Living in the illusion causes us to neglect the life God has given. It's like living in the plot of the movie *The Matrix*. The characters in this film were plugged into a computer that created the illusion of their thoughts being real. They didn't have real lives. Their bodies were dying from atrophy and neglect because they were living in an illusion, though they believed it to be real. They didn't realize that the illusion was the one thing that enslaved them to the matrix and alienated them from real life.

Choosing life on the mindplane is like choosing to live in the matrix. We think we are living, but we are not! When living in the mindplane, our hope of becoming places the attainment of our goal someplace in the future. The hope of a future me distracts me from the *now*. God only exists in the now. The power of God can only be experienced in the NOW! God is giving me life at this very moment. The illusion causes me to look to the external instead of the internal. The hope of who I will become blinds me to who I am. I create the delusion that I have needs, based on my past life. I look to the future for God's victory. And I totally neglect the victory that I have when I look to my inner man.

In his attempt to encourage women, Peter said:

Do not let your adornment be merely outward; arranging the hair, wearing gold, or putting on fine apparel; rather let it be the hidden person of the heart, with the incorruptible beauty of a gentle and quiet spirit, which is very precious in the sight of God (1 Peter 3:3-4).

He was not discouraging outward adornments. He was simply saying that we should place our focus for identity and beauty on the inner man—the hidden man of the heart. To look to the inner you, the righteous you, you have to look into your heart now!

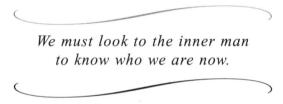

*We must look to the inner man
to know who we are now.*

Instead of looking in the mirror to know who we are, we need to look to the hundreds of identity scriptures in the Word of God. Then we will see ourselves in a whole new light. Reading those scriptures about who we are and what we have will give us the basis to consider God's truth as our reality. It will point our faith to the real source instead of to the illusion of the mindplane.

Paul said it like this in Ephesians 4:23-24:

Be renewed in the spirit of your mind, and...put on the new man which was created according to God, in true righteousness and holiness.

Renewing your mind, changing the way you see yourself, is the process whereby you put on the new you, the inward you. It doesn't create the new you; it puts you in connection with the new you. Paul clearly told us that by changing the way we think we can put on the new man...right now! By following this process, we will, at the same time, automatically put off the person we were. Our problem is never that we need to become. Our challenge is that we need to believe and act on the reality instead of the illusion.

In his letter to Philemon, Paul wrote, *"That the communication of thy faith may become effectual by the acknowledging of every good thing which is in you in Christ Jesus"* (verse 6, KJV). Religion never tells you to acknowledge who you are. It never tells you to see, notice, and acknowledge the good things. It tells you to notice and fix the bad things. It tells you that you really are the old you trying to get good enough to please God. As noble as this may sound, this concept will only lead you on a journey into worship of self, a religion of deceit that totally denies the finished work of Jesus.

As you consider the good things about yourself in Jesus to be real, it will renew your mind. It will change your focus from the illusion of becoming to the reality of being. The power of God will take you through a metamorphism that will bring the rest of your being in line with your internal reality.

As a believer, you will look somewhere for your sense of reality and identity. You may look to your past, which is an illusion—the memories of a dead person. You may look to the external present, which is legalism. Or you may look to the hidden man of the heart, which is in Christ. This is the only way to escape the worldly concept of change and enter into the Kingdom experience of transformation.

Here are some things to consider and do to change the focus of your view.

1. Is my view of me based on the resurrected Jesus or on my past?

2. Will I accept God's view of me as my reality? Do I know what God says about me?

3. Write ten identity scriptures on cards and keep them with you for thirty days.

4. Memorize these scriptures.

5. Every time you have a self-thought that is inconsistent with these scriptures, correct yourself internally and make a bold statement, "In Jesus I am...." Insert those scriptures to complete this statement.

CHAPTER FIFTEEN

THE ETERNAL NOW

Issues of time and eternity have long presented a spiritual and scientific struggle for man. Having spent our entire life controlled by the laws of time and space, we have created a finite sense of reality that fits the reasoning of our carnal mind. Although grasping these laws is essential for life in this natural world, they blind us to a greater reality that is sustained by laws that supersede our understanding.

Time is a created phenomenon. It only exists on our plane. Time is also an experienced phenomenon. When we lay this human body down, we will never again experience time. Some studies seem to indicate that our capacity to experience time changes as we grow older. When we are young, time seems to stand still. As we age, it seems to fly past. The natural mind is controlled by the time-space phenomenon and seeks to understand God within these restricted limitations, thereby reducing God and our experience of Him to something much less than He presents Himself to be.

God dwells in the eternal now! He is not the God of yesterday. Nor is He the God of tomorrow. He is simply God. The patriarchs of the Old Testament avoided limiting God to time by calling Him "the God of our fathers." In so doing they referred to a time in the past when their fathers were alive on earth, but did not relegate God to a particular time and space. They knew He was omnipresent. They understood that He did not exist in the framework of time and space as they knew it.

The Sadducees struggled with eternal concepts. Therefore they created doctrines to justify their reasoning. Like many groups today, they denied the resurrection. Matthew recorded Jesus' encounter with the Sadducees, telling how He confounded them with this quote from Exodus, *"'I am the God of Abraham, the God of Isaac, and the God of Jacob'? God is not the God of the dead, but of the living"* (Matthew 22:32). In so saying He not only made God timeless, but He also made man timeless.

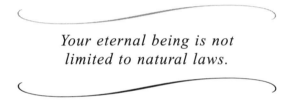

*Your eternal being is not
limited to natural laws.*

We also are eternal beings, yet we live in a natural body. Our body is limited to the laws that govern this natural plane of existence. But our inner man is eternal and should be freed from the natural laws to live the *"law of the Spirit of life in Christ Jesus"* (Romans 8:2). As spirit-beings, we have entered a new realm called the Kingdom of God. It functions by an entirely different set of rules than this natural world. But our ability to function in that realm is determined by our acceptance of a new reality—faith in God's Word!

Because we choose carnality, our mind is set on understanding all things from a natural perspective. In his outstanding letter to the Romans, Paul explained the plight of the person who attempts to live according to the dictates of the natural mind.

For those who live according to the flesh set their minds on the things of the flesh, but those who live according to the Spirit, the things of the Spirit. For to be carnally minded is death, but to be spiritually minded is life and peace. Because the carnal mind is enmity against God; for it is not subject to the law of God, nor indeed can be. So then, those who are in the flesh cannot please God (Romans 8:5-8).

You can't make spiritual realities fit into the reasoning of the natural mind or the limitations of the natural world. The natural mind is how one navigates the terrain of the natural world. But it creates a blinding perspective for Kingdom realities.

As eternal beings we too must live in the now. We must seek to experience God and His power at this moment. Our tendency is to live in the past or in the future, both of which are illusions that keep us from living in the now!

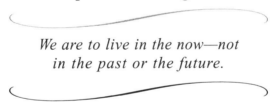

We are to live in the now—not in the past or the future.

God is the great I Am. He is not the "I was" or the "I will." He is the I Am. As such, He can only be experienced in the present tense. When we base our experience with God on a past event, we lose touch with the power of His presence. When we place our hope in a future experience, we deny the reality of His power now.

There is much to be said about the presence of God. His presence brings the supernatural. His presence brings peace. His presence brings the experience of all that He is.

Of all the factors of His presence that have been taught, the one that seems to be most neglected is that His presence is present tense! You can't experience His presence any time except now.

By entering this realm called the Kingdom of God, we begin to function closer to the plane God intends for us. In the Old Testament, God's presence was manifest. It was something that the believer had to wait on and prepare for. In the Kingdom realm, His presence can be experienced any time we choose to be present! We are never waiting on Him.

I often hear people speak of that special time in the future when they will experience what they need from God. But the New Testament says, *"'In an acceptable time I have heard you, and in the day of salvation I have helped you.' Behold, now is the accepted time; behold, now is the day of salvation"* (2 Corinthians 6:2). The special time for God is now! The special time for you is now!

So many people cannot live in the now. We have become masters at business. We must have our mind occupied with external clutter because we fear the now. Beneath the layers of unresolved issues, abounding fears, and low self-worth is a reality that is beyond anything we have ever known—the new me! We seem inept or unwilling to settle our minds, direct our attention, and experience life as it is happening. We are always on our way to somewhere. And we'll get there someday. We convince ourselves that we will enjoy tomorrow. The problem is, when tomorrow gets here, it becomes today, and we don't know how to experience today.

Much of our praying is about what we want at some point in the future. We usually want it now. But we expect it in the future. We think that at some time in the future God will reward our praying and grant our request. R.C.H. Lenski does such a great job of explaining how faith abides in the present tense. Mark 11:24 says, *"Therefore I say to you, whatever things you ask when you pray, believe that you receive them, and you will have them."* Lenski, based on the tenses of the verbs, translates this as *"Go on believing that you did receive."* He says:

> The aorist ἐλάβετε "did receive" seems strange and is yet perfectly in order, especially with πιστευτε, "go on believing." The disciples were to go on believing while they are praying that God has already granted their prayer, which will appear in due time even as Jesus now adds: "and you shall have it...."[1]

Jesus is in us now. His promises are now. The past is settled. It is over. The old you is dead and needs nothing. At the resurrection, the Lord Jesus received all things for life and godliness. At your new birth, all that He has and is came into you. The future is an illusion that may or may not occur. Everything about God is now. We are taught to believe that we have received. Although the manifestation in this natural realm may not occur at the present time, we take possession now. I call this the power of the present tense. What is it that makes us want to push everything with God into the future? No doubt a small part of it is simply unbelief! But I believe there is an even greater issue.

In order for me to receive something now that cannot be seen in this natural realm, I must be alive to God in my heart. And I must be in touch with the inner man—who is

---

1. R.C.H. Lenski, *The Interpretation of Mark's Gospel* (Minneapolis, Minnesota: Augsburg Publishing House, 1946), pp. 495-496.

in touch with God. Our inability to connect with God in the present tense is merely a reflection of our inability to know ourselves in the present. The new you is experienced in the heart and in the present tense.

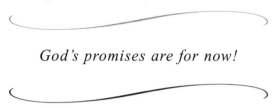

God's promises are for now!

As I actually get to know the hidden man of my heart—the me that is created in righteousness—I end my struggle to become and I accept the reality of being. I no longer seek God to give. I thank God that I have. I am freed from the limits of the man of the past. I no longer look to become in the future. I am in the eternal now. My hope is no longer in a future time. It is in an eternal being.

When I stop striving for change, I free myself to experience transformation...painless, positive, permanent, effortless change. Live in the eternal now, and free yourself from the limitation of the past and the illusion of the future.

1. Begin to remind yourself that you are an eternal being!

2. Every time you think of the person you would like to become, remind yourself that inwardly you already are that person. You have those traits.

3. Every time you think of a need, remind yourself that the solution is already yours in Jesus.

4. Make it a daily practice to acknowledge who you are in Jesus.

5. Determine to lose any sense of self other than your new identity in Jesus.

CHAPTER SIXTEEN

THE TREASURE

I once heard a renowned business consultant ask a group of people, "What would it be worth for me to show you thousands, if not millions, of dollars in revenues you could be getting from your current business that you are now overlooking?" Like any great salesperson, he attempted to lead the group into a level of positive expectancy, while they endeavored to remain calm and cautious.

As he continued with his innovative ideas, which were very sound business principles, I likened his task to what happens when a person walks into my church services. My task is similar to his. All I'm trying to do is get a person to see what benefits they already have and make the necessary adjustment to begin living in those benefits. If they are lost, they need to know that Jesus already paid the price. If they are saved, they need to know that everything God has for them is already in them.

However, people tend to hear from their sense of self-worth. When I talk about participation in resources you already have, I am talking about *being*. In their diminished state of self-worth, though, my listeners are hearing, "This is what you have to *do*."

At one particular seminar, the conversations I heard at the break confirmed what I suspected. Most of the people were being told one thing, but were hearing something else. I wondered as I listened throughout the rest of the day, "How many people will actually put any of this into practice?" The water cooler discussions had already indicated a large number who would do little or nothing because they misunderstood the message.

Studies indicate that of the people who attend business or self-help seminars, few ever apply what they learn. Those who try may be as low as ten percent. As I sat listening to this extraordinary business consultant unfold his plan, I knew it was good advice. There was no doubt in my mind that it would work because I had already applied much of it.

As the speaker went on, my mind raced to the many pastors I work with who want to reach more people. They want to become more successful, but they seldom go beyond their current levels of effectiveness. Most people reach a success level that becomes comfortable for them, and it soon becomes a boundary they will never cross. No matter how much help or information they are given, they will seldom rise above their current success.

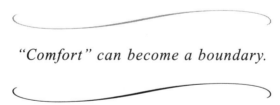

"Comfort" can become a boundary.

The writer of Proverbs said, *"Keep your heart with all diligence, for out of it spring the issues of life"* (Proverbs 4:23). The word *issues* could be translated, "boundaries." From this verse, we realize it's not the information we know that will make us successful, even though it *is* a factor. Instead, the boundaries that emerge from our heart will determine our level of success. This is why people who win lotteries are usually broke in just a few years. They don't have a heart for success. Their boundaries have already been established.

Marty came to my office frustrated and ready to give up. She was a young businesswoman who was struggling with success, or should I say the lack of success? She was having trouble applying the business principles she had learned. In fact, every time she learned a new business tip and tried to put it to work, it would usually fall far short of her anticipated goals. Marty's theme statement became, "I don't understand!"

I tried to help Marty understand that her need for transformation was greater than her need for information. I explained that her lack of success was directly related to her lack of experiencing Jesus in her heart. She resisted my input and indicated that I was being a little over spiritual by even suggesting that a business problem could have its roots in spiritual issues.

I tried to help her understand. "This is not about doing business. This is about being the person you want to be." Marty's business failures, like most people's, were the product of her sense of self. She didn't see herself as being a successful person. Her attempts at becoming caused her more pain than success. She had spent thousands of dollars attending seminars attempting to become a success. But she had not yet tapped into the power of being!

Because I presented a persuasive argument, she could not completely deny what I said, but the conversation ended with, "I don't understand!" At the risk of being rude, I took Marty's hand, looked her in the eye, and gently said, "Marty, this proves my point. Understanding is an issue of the heart. You have plenty of great information, but you don't have the heart to apply it. The way you see yourself prevents you from understanding how to apply what you've learned!"

Once again Marty left my office in a state of confusion. She was on her way to spend another thousand dollars to attend yet another seminar that would be filled with useful information that she would probably not be able to successfully apply. She, like most people I deal with, thought more knowledge was the answer.

Marty had made the crucial mistake. She had looked everywhere for help except within. She was overlooking her greatest resource: Christ in her. She was like the business people in the seminar I attended. She had incredible resources that she had never tapped into. Her greatest resource would be her new identity in Christ. If only she would put her effort into *being*, instead of *becoming*, she would experience the transformation of her sense of self. Instead she spent all of her energy trying to get more external information rather than yielding to internal power.

The apostle Paul said, *"We have this treasure in jars of clay to show that this all-surpassing power is from God and not from us"* (2 Corinthians 4:7, NIV). Every believer in the world has untapped resources. Not only are these resources untapped, they also are unlimited. We have the life and power of God in us. That power can manifest at any moment to energize us to live all our dreams. But it is more about being than doing.

Too often we only associate God's power in us as an ability to do things. Although that is partially true, God wants our *doing* to emerge from our *being*. He is far more interested in what you are than He is in what you do! In Philippians 2:13, Paul said, *"For it is God who works in you both to will and to do for His good pleasure."* The will to do something emerges from the ability to choose or determine. Choices are made from who you are. Those godly choices are then energized by "Christ in you." The power to do is destructive without the character to choose!

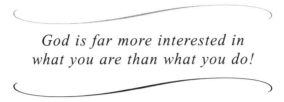

*God is far more interested in
what you are than what you do!*

There is a mystery around which all the Gospel actually works: *"Christ in you, the hope of glory"* (Colossians 1:27). The living awareness that Christ is living in your heart is the key to engaging a Bible-based sense of dignity and worth. It is the foundation upon which we stand as priests and kings. Without this as an abiding reality, all else becomes dead works.

According to the book of Genesis, man originally ruled and reigned over all of planet Earth. We mistakenly think that was simply a matter of power. But man's ability to do the work emerged from his sense of self. Hebrews 2:7-8 gives us insight into the prerequisite for living like royalty: a divine sense of dignity and worth. *"You have crowned him with glory and honor, and set him over the works of Your hands. You have put all things in subjection under his feet."* It was without question man's sense of dignity and worth emerging from his connection with God that empowered him to rule and reign!

Man lost his divine connection at the fall. But Christ not only recreated a divine connection; He also came to live in us. He gave us a connection that Adam, Abraham, Moses, and even King David never knew. Our sense of self-worth should far exceed anything any Old Testament patriarch ever experienced.

People who are not experiencing "Christ in you" have somehow missed the essence of the New Testament. This is the mystery that was hidden from all previous ages. This is the apex of Christianity. Without accepting this revelation as a living reality, all else is simply information.

Christ in you is the unlimited resource for self-worth and personal power. Christ is the resource that abides in every believer, yet so few draw upon Him. Our awareness of this truth is the prerequisite for power. This is the key to the confidence and faith to walk in every promise of God. This is the root of every positive, healthy emotion. This is the ultimate in being the person you want to be. This very awareness moves a person from his need to become to his realization of being! We are who we are in direct proportion to our sense of "Christ in me"!

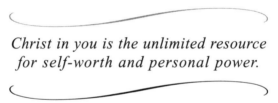

Christ in you is the unlimited resource for self-worth and personal power.

Make every effort to connect to Jesus in you. It will transform your potential into power! It is the treasure that all seek and few find! To begin, respond to the following:

1. Do you have an abiding awareness of Christ in you?

2. What are the things you do that tend to stimulate this awareness?

3. List five things you could do to increase your awareness of Christ in you.[1]

---

1. Heart Physics® is a thirty-day program designed to give you an abiding sense of Christ in you and to bring you to a realization of limitlessness through Jesus. Go to www.heartphysics.com for more information.

4.   How will you incorporate these steps into your life?

5.   When will you start?

CHAPTER SEVENTEEN

THE SENSUAL BELIEVER

Jesus often made the statement, *"He who has ears to hear, let him hear."* The meaning of this statement is obvious, but there is also a more subtle revelation we can gather from it. Hearing with our physical ears is not the only hearing we're capable of. There is a deeper kind of hearing—a hearing in the Spirit. This is true of each of our natural senses.

We have both internal and external senses. The five natural senses are mirrored with at least the same five internal senses. We've heard biblical phrases like, "hear the voice of the Spirit," or "taste and see that the Lord is good." And there is the "sweet savor," which reflects smell. Then there is "seeing in the Spirit."

The five natural senses are indispensable for living and functioning in this natural world. They are the receptors through which we experience the natural. When we die, our body dies, and thus we lose the senses that kept us in touch with this world. Likewise, our internal senses allow us to be in touch with the other-than-physical world.

We know the natural senses can be heightened with use and diminished with neglect. The "old man," the old you who was crucified with Christ, lived by external or natural senses. Thus, he was carnal (natural) or sensual. As such, he was not alive or aware of God. As a new creature born of the Spirit, we should begin to live by our spiritual senses. We should develop them at least as much as our carnal (natural) senses.

When a person loses his natural sight, he relies on his sense of sound. By exercise he heightens this ability far beyond what he ever knew was possible. He had this latent potential all along, but due to a total dependence on sight he had never developed it.

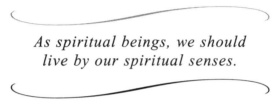

As spiritual beings, we should live by our spiritual senses.

Likewise, we have the ability to develop our internal senses, but we rarely do so. Just as the person who loses sight has to go though the trial and error of developing new senses, we too must practice developing and depending on our spiritual senses. The senses we use to guide our life, whether natural or spiritual, will be the ones we have developed and learned to rely on.

Developing the spiritual senses is done through prayer, reading the Word, and listening for and meditating on the Lord. When asked about the secret of his success, Dr. David (Paul) Yongii Cho simply replied, "I pray. I obey." That just seems too simple. Yet, there is not a better recipe for success. If in fact you can hear the voice of the Lord, you know what to obey. Most believers do not hear God in their heart. They simply decide what they will do and ask God to bless it. In our mysticism, we somehow think that if we simply add "in the name of Jesus" to the end of a statement, it becomes the will of God.

Most of our decisions are made from a carnal, sensual perspective. Through our memories, we draw upon the resource of our old man, combine it with the stimuli provided by our five natural senses, and apply our personal logic to it, and the formula is complete. Then, of course, we do it in the name of Jesus. Those who have a more serious commitment to God might actually attempt to mix the Word of God into this formula. But in the end, this is still a carnal, sensual attempt at duplicating the wisdom of God. This show of wisdom is not from God! *"This wisdom does not descend from above, but is earthly, sensual, demonic"* (James 3:15).

In my early walk with God, I wanted to hear and know the voice of God in my heart. I made it a lifelong practice to read, study, and meditate in the Word of God. But in those early days, I also made fasting a regular practice. I found that as I ignored or mortified the deeds of my flesh, it heightened my internal senses. *"For if ye live after the flesh, ye shall die: but if ye through the Spirit do mortify the deeds of the body, ye shall live"* (Romans 8:13, KJV). Fasting is one way to take the fast track to developing your inner senses. It turns your attention inward to the voice of the Spirit.

Learning to hear with my inner man has been and continues to be the adventure of a lifetime! It is something I continue to practice as a way of life. According to Strong's, the word *deeds* could be translated as "practice."[1] Any time we use our senses, we are not simply taking an action. We are exercising and strengthening those senses and becoming more proficient in their use.

---

1.   NT:4234: "praxis (prax'-is); from NT:4238; practice, i.e. (concretely) an act; by extension, a function" (Biblesoft's *New Exhaustive Strong's Numbers and Concordance with Expanded Greek-Hebrew Dictionary*. Copyright © 1994, 2003 Biblesoft, Inc. and International Bible Translators, Inc.).

The carnal person is a person who depends on his natural senses to make spiritual decisions. Every decision that exercises his natural senses tends to cause him to neglect his internal senses. Thus the Bible calls this type of person sensual and carnal.

A carnal person depends on his natural senses to make a spiritual decision.

In Matthew 13:14-16, Jesus explained why He used parables:

And in them the prophecy of Isaiah is fulfilled, which says: "Hearing you will hear and shall not understand, and seeing you will see and not perceive; for the hearts of this people have grown dull. Their ears are hard of hearing, and their eyes they have closed, lest they should see with their eyes and hear with their ears, lest they should understand with their hearts and turn, so that I should heal them."

Jesus was not trying to hide the truth from these people. But He spoke the truth in such a way that those who had developed their internal senses could perceive it. But in so doing, it also meant that those who relied solely on their natural, carnal senses could not perceive it.

Spiritual understanding and perception are capacities of the heart. But we attempt to know God through our flesh. We want spiritual things to make sense in a way that somehow preserves and gratifies our old natural man. But this will never happen. You will never know, understand or please God through the use of the natural senses. The western world has so externalized the Bible to make it palatable to our senses that we have all but lost the internal essence. To develop our capacity to actually know God, we must develop our inner man.

When talking about our capacity to grasp an understanding of righteousness, the Bible says in Hebrews 5:14:

> *But solid food belongs to those who are of full age, that is, those who by reason of use have their senses exercised to discern both good and evil.*

The term *senses* refers to their ability to perceive. The person who never develops his inner senses cannot grasp or perceive the eternal realities of God. His concept of God is based on rules and formulas, performance and carnality. He lives in the flesh!

You must develop your spiritual senses in order to grasp the eternal realities of God.

The flesh is the natural man. It is any aspect of the natural man attempting to know God, relate to God, understand God, or please God. The flesh and the old man are the same thing. Trying to live right, do right, or be righteous by will power, self-control, observance of rules, or ceremonies is an effort to reconcile the flesh (the old you) to God. The old you has been crucified and cannot be made right with God. Any attempt to make the old you right with God puts you in a realm where it is *"impossible to please Him"*[2] because you would be in the flesh!

---

2.   See Hebrews 11:6.

Paul showed that the flesh and the old man are the same. In Galatians 2:20 and Romans 6:6 he refered to the old man being crucified with Christ. In Galatians 5:24, he called it the flesh: *"And those who are Christ's have crucified the flesh with its passions and desires."* Understanding this subtle reality can be the gateway to a life of resurrection power.

Our old man doesn't need counseling. He needs ignoring. He can't do enough deeds to become acceptable to God. He has died the death we deserved for our sin. We need to give up all the memories and accept the new realities. Jesus said, *"That which is born of the flesh is flesh, and that which is born of the Spirit is spirit"* (John 3:6). We've got to decide where we will put our attention. Which set of senses will we develop—natural or spiritual? Which senses will we use to direct our life? Do we want the wisdom from above or the wisdom that is based on our natural senses?

There is a war that goes on in the mind: the war of flesh against the Spirit.

> *For the flesh lusts against the Spirit, and the Spirit against the flesh; and these are contrary to one another, so that you do not do the things that you wish* (Galatians 5:17).

Our problem is not the devil. Our struggle occurs when the external and internal senses are in conflict.

Will we try to live a spiritual life based on the natural senses, or will we develop the senses of the inner man? *"Those who live according to the flesh set their minds on the things of the flesh, but those who live according to the Spirit, the things of the Spirit"* (Romans 8:5). Will we continue to live by a logic that was developed in the absence of God?

God has created us to be a new man who is already righteous, holy, sanctified, anointed, and blessed. When we attempt to get God to give us anointing, we are unwittingly saying, "I don't believe and accept that the new me has been raised up with Jesus. I want You to anoint the old me." In a pious attempt at righteousness, we commit, "I promise to make the old me live good enough to deserve it."

Any attempt to get from God what He has already given through the Lord Jesus is a negotiation to keep the old man alive. It is our attempt to make our old man worthy enough to receive the inheritance. Every effort to keep the old man alive heightens our sensual tendencies. It ignores and diminishes our spiritual senses. It pulls our focus from the spiritual to the natural and draws us further from God. We are in essence, therefore, achieving the opposite of our intent!

Jesus said that we've got to pick up our cross if we want to follow Him. We've got to let the old man fall to the ground and die. We've got to die to self. The old man does not want to die! Some part of us are so afraid of trusting God, of giving up what we have known, that we ignore the resurrection life and continue to "fix up" the old man. We must let him die so we can begin to live!

When your senses are alive to who you used to be, your mind always leads you to think that you must "become." Through habit, you then fall into the vain attempt to turn that person into who you want to be. Thus the self-destructive syndrome of becoming is initiated. When you accept the death of the old you, you are forced to rely on the spiritual senses. When that happens you are connected to the new you. Then you settle into "being." You enter the eternal now and release the new you into your life.

You can experience metamorphism...the process of transformation right now.

1. What do you do to develop your inner senses?

2. Are you confident that you can hear and sense God's direction?

3. Spend an hour with God. Let it go where it goes. But continually bring your attention back to the fact that this is time with you and God.

4. When you sense an inner impulse, step away from the activity that is demanding your attention. Pray. Listen and see if God is speaking.

5. Is your sense of who you are in Christ as real as your sense of who you were?

6. When making decisions, let the external indicators be the last considerations.

CHAPTER EIGHTEEN

THE CARNAL ADDICTION

Living in carnality is an addiction, just as surely as the constant use of cocaine, heroin, or alcohol is an addiction. This is why it's so difficult for people to break free from the dark, sultry clutches of carnality. And like all addictions, the more socially acceptable it becomes, the more normal it seems. After more than thirty years of experience with substance abuse counseling, I've found it more than obvious that carnality is an addiction that mirrors all the patterns of drug or alcohol addiction. Yet, carnality is applauded in the Church. It is often unwittingly interpreted and rewarded as spirituality because it satisfies our need to feel good about ourselves.

Carnality is an addiction just like drug and alcohol addictions.

We all have a desire to experience a fulfilled, satisfied life. Yet fulfillment is often confused with happiness, and many people pursue those things that create positive feelings in them. People who have not been taught don't know what to do to create and maintain positive emotions. For some, substance abuse provides the kinds of positive emotions they crave. Others gain positive emotions through personal development. Their use of regular exercise, proper diet, emotional management techniques, and a predictable spiritual routine stimulate an abundance of positive, healthy emotions.

Then there are others—the selfish, lazy, or greedy—who are not willing to put forth the effort. They settle for staying as they are. And finally, there are those who don't believe fulfillment can be obtained. All of these people are living in a form of carnality. They are either searching for an alternative to God's plan for fulfillment or they have stopped searching all together.

Those who are still searching but attempting to reach fulfillment through natural means are headed for the wrong goal. The carnal pursuit of happiness is a journey into sensuality. It does not lead to spiritual fulfillment. Through substances, sex, or ego, these people are in pursuit of an alternative to the life that God offers. The apostle John said it like this: *"For all that is in the world; the lust of the flesh, the lust of the eyes, and the pride of life; is not of the Father but is of the world"* (1 John 2:16).

The world system does have something to offer. It will create pleasure for a moment, but it will alienate you from "Christ in you " as your source. It will rob you of the power of transformation and plunge you into dead works, legalism, and ritualism.

The world system offers alternatives and substitutes for Jesus' promise of an abundant life. But in the end, those alternatives become destructive addictions that steal from you all they promise to give. The writer of Proverbs described it like this: *"There is a way that seems right to a man, but its end is the way of death"* (Proverbs 14:12). The more socially acceptable something becomes, the more it seems right!

Anything that gives us pleasure through the five senses has the potential to become a destructive addiction. The five senses must be stimulated to cause the brain to release the endorphins, natural pleasure stimulators, into the body. The release of these pleasure stimulators causes a feeling of euphoria, excitement, or sexual stimulation. These pleasure stimulators can be released by sex, drugs, pornography, danger, power, or any external stimuli.

Although the five senses can be used in a positive, healthy manner, they also can create an addictive potential when coupled with other emotional or spiritual factors. On a physical or emotional level, we develop a tolerance or familiarity with certain stimuli. When that happens we need more…more drugs, more pornography, more self-improvement seminars, more immersion into religious activity, more of whatever we use to stimulate ourselves.

The worse part hasn't even happened yet. When we begin to deny our body these pleasure endorphins, we no longer have an adequate ability to feel good in normal life. In time we need the stimulation, not just to feel euphoric, but simply to feel normal. This is devastating when we apply this to our spiritual life.

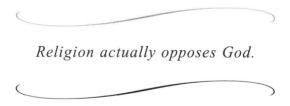

Religion actually opposes God.

Religion is carnal and external; it is based on natural factors. As Paul said, it is not subject to the law of life in

Christ. Moreover, it opposes God.[1] It is an addiction. It relies on external stimulation to feel God. People have what they consider to be spiritual experiences. Yet, they don't grow. Those experiences do not make them more emotionally stable. They do not develop their character. This is the beginning of a cycle that consumes their entire life.

If we equate stimulation to a spiritual experience, we have now defined spirituality. Since we want to be spiritual, we will pursue what we have defined as spiritual. After a particular song or experience stimulates my five senses, it begins to take more of the same type of stimulation to make me feel spiritual (euphoric). Like a junkie searching for his next fix, we are craving another experience so we can feel spiritual.

If this is our definition of spirituality, then this is what we will seek when we face life's challenges. This is why some people live from special meeting to special meeting. They need the "fix" to make them feel that God is near. In time, religious activity overtakes real life. We don't have time to be who Christ has made us to be. We neglect our families, our friendships, and all the healthy components of a truly spiritual life in the quest for another spiritual experience. It robs us of our real life! But it is socially applauded in religious circles. Come to church more. Pray more. Do more religious works. That is always the answer in a religious environment.

I have seen junkies sell their automobiles for pennies on the dollar. They will sell a $500 television for a $20 dollar "fix." They give away the things that bring comfort and

---

1.   Romans 8:7: *"Because the carnal mind is enmity against God; for it is not subject to the law of God, nor indeed can be."*

sell themselves into a life of destitution. I also see believers give away their lives as they pursue false spirituality. They abandon character development. They sometimes neglect their families. They trade off the things in life that could bring real comfort, peace, and fulfillment in exchange for a few minutes of euphoria.

There is nothing wrong with having experiences. We are emotional beings—we need healthy, positive emotional experiences. But our belief system will determine if these experiences point us inward to Christ in us or outward in search of a God who is far away.

If we live in the external carnal world of religion, then an experience is over when it's over! A truly spiritual experience, however, always becomes part of our transformation. It moves what is inside our heart to the outside where it affects our body, our health, our thoughts, our emotions, our character, and our ability to be the person we want to be.

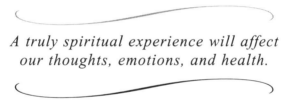

A truly spiritual experience will affect our thoughts, emotions, and health.

In James' letter to a church that had grown exorbitantly carnal, he warned the believers not to become forgetful hearers of the Word. The Message Bible does an excellent job of translating this passage:

Don't fool yourself into thinking that you are a listener when you are anything but, letting the Word go in one ear and out the other. Act on what you hear! Those who hear and don't act are like those who glance in the mirror, walk away, and two minutes later have no idea who they are, what they look like (James 1:22-24, MSG).

This describes a person who hears spiritual truth from the Word of God, but doesn't apply it on a heart-level. Likewise, it could describe someone who has an experience. If we only experience God's Word through our intellect or on an emotional level, then the truths we heard are gone when the experience subsides. We have taken what could have been a new phase of transformation and allowed it to become part of our carnal addiction.

But the doer of the Word is a different kind of person all together. The term *doer of the word* is far more than someone who simply puts what he hears into practice. The word *doer* could be translated, "poetic performer."[2] A poetic performer is a person who doesn't merely read the lines of the poem; he adds emotion and imagination to them. They become believable and real as he expresses them with his entire being!

A person who confesses or meditates on the Word of God, adding his emotion and imagination to it, influences his own heart! When he hears the Word, he doesn't just listen and walk away. He listens and combines it with faith and reflective thought; he emotionally acknowledges it. He makes it part of the fabric of his life. He sees himself in the Word. It becomes a part of his identity.

James continued:

For if anyone is a hearer of the word and not a doer [poetic performer], *he is like a man observing his natural face in a mirror; for he observes himself, goes away, and*

---

2. "poietes (poy-ay-tace'); from NT:4160; a performer; specifically, a "poet"; KJV – doer, poet." (Biblesoft's *New Exhaustive Strong's Numbers and Concordance with Expanded Greek-Hebrew Dictionary*. Copyright © 1994, 2003 Biblesoft, Inc. and International Bible Translators, Inc.).

immediately forgets what kind of man he was (James 1:23-24).

Imagine if you were severely disfigured by an accident of some kind and because of this you were self-conscious about your appearance. It affects everything you do. In every conversation you wonder what people think about you. If you are attracted to someone, you immediately shut out that emotion for fear of being rejected.

Now suppose that one day you are able to receive reconstructive surgery. You look in the mirror and find the change so wonderful that it's hard to believe. While gazing into that mirror, you feel incredible. You are having an emotional experience. Then, with your new appearance, you determine to create a new social life. You buy new clothes. You get a new hairstyle, and you head out into the social world. But every time you encounter a new person, you feel all of the old feelings you had before the surgery. Why? You've forgotten that you have a new face. You should feel right about yourself. But you don't because you keep forgetting that you look completely different now.

According to Lenski, James was really writing that when you look in the mirror of "the law of liberty" you see the "face of your birth."[3] That is exactly what we should do every time we read the Word, every time we have an experience, every time we encounter God. We should look into our hearts, at Christ in us, and we should ask, "How does this make me look, in light of my new birth?" Then we should behold that new identity. We should acknowledge it to God. We should praise, worship, meditate, and acknowledge that

---

3.   R.C.H. Lenski, *The Interpretation of the Epistle to the Hebrews and the Epistle of James* (Minneapolis, Minnesota: Augsburg Publishing House, 1966), p. 555.

reality until it has become an indelible part of our life's fabric! We should lose every sense of who we used to be. We should have no thought about ourselves that is not based on this new man in the mirror.

Then when we walk away and face life's challenges, we don't feel the need to run back and get another religious fix. We remember who we are. We act accordingly. This is the heart of *being* instead of *doing*. This is the ultimate secret to becoming the person we want to be in a positive, painless, permanent, effortless manner. Being always leads to doing. The person we want to be will always make the right decisions and do the right things when acting out of our new identity, the new man.

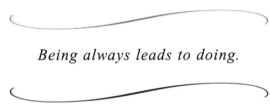

Being always leads to doing.

If we depend on experiences that stimulate our emotions, we will go from mountaintop to valley and back again. Life will be a never-ending emotional rollercoaster. When we will look into the *"perfect law of liberty,"* we will be transformed from glory to glory. When transformed, religious activities will not overtake our life. We will be a witness. We will do the things that are natural for a person who lives from his identity. We will fulfill the call of God and live our personal dreams.

Answer the following questions to begin throwing off carnal responses.

1. Do you depend on experiences to make you feel right about yourself and God?

2. Do your experiences fade with time and grow weaker?

3. Do your experiences make you grow stronger in your sense of identity in Christ?

4. Begin to allow every experience to cause you to look inward and to remind you of who you are in Jesus!

5. Make it a practice to create a sense of who you are in Jesus before you make any major decisions.

CHAPTER NINETEEN

MATH OR MIRACLES

Marty, whom we talked about earlier, struggled under a destructive paradox. She knew she didn't feel right about herself. But she also knew that the more she tried to develop a sense of self-worth, the worse she felt about herself. Everything I tried to do to help her only magnified her shortcomings in her own mind.

Then I shared with Marty the principles of *laboring to enter into rest!* To her it just sounded like laboring. "How can I work any harder? This sounds like dead works to me!" she insisted. I encouraged her to try it. "You've tried everything else," I said. "Just use Heart Physics® for a week and see what changes." I finally convinced her. Reluctantly she agreed to try it. After one week, a light began to shine through her darkness and her understanding grew.

Until then, Marty had been working math instead of miracles. Marty, like so many believers, couldn't grasp the paradox of transformation. Change emphasizes becoming. Transformation puts the focus on being. People mistakenly think, "If I 'am,' then I don't have to do anything." That's why the writer of Hebrews clarified the issue.[1] You do have to labor! But, you're not laboring to become. You're laboring to convince yourself of the truth about who you are in Christ! As much as you believe "you are" is the degree to

---

1.   See Hebrews 4:11.

which you will experience transformation into being. Everything else is just math.

One day Marty blurted out, "I don't know what you're talking about when you say 'everything else is just math'!" That's when I explained the choice between math and miracles. You see, transformation is the destiny of man. We are all predestined to become like Jesus.[2] Therefore, resisting growth and transformation is resisting God. The purpose of growth is not to fix what we perceive to be wrong with us. We grow because we want to experience the limitless depths of God's love and goodness. We grow because everything around us is changing. To experience a continual quality of life, we must continually develop.

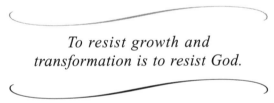

To resist growth and transformation is to resist God.

For most people growth is a matter of math. They either add something to their lives or they subtract something from their lives. When people think of growth, they tend to ask, "What do I need to make my life better?" Or, "What do I need to add?" This kind of thinking immediately focuses you on what you're lacking. Our sense of lack is deceptive in that it leads to codependency, sin, and destructive behavior.[3]

Sometimes we look at our lives and conclude that we need to subtract something in order to grow. The idea of eliminating something creates the fear of lack. And our fear

---

2.   See Romans 8:29-30.

3.   For more on this topic, read my book *Breaking the Cycle* (Huntsville, Alabama: Milestones International Publishing, 2003).

increases the possibility of having a negative experience, thereby creating the expectation of pain. As a rule, people tend to resist anything painful. The dread of pain drives us to postpone change.

If growth comes by taking away something we viewed as pleasing, we are unlikely to sustain our change. In times of difficulty we tend to seek pleasure. That's when we fall back on the enjoyable things we gave up in order to grow.

Change by math is better than nothing, but it doesn't fit my criteria for miraculous transformation...positive, painless, permanent, and effortless! Change comes by adding or subtracting. Transformation comes by being! Since you can't increase being, this means that you can only increase your awareness of being. This is where the laboring comes in.

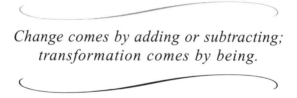

Change comes by adding or subtracting; transformation comes by being.

Marty then tapped into the oldest power tool in the entire Bible: meditation. Biblical meditation is the only promise we have of transformation. In the parable about the sower and the seed, Jesus explained that the amount of study and meditation we spend on God's Word is the same amount of life that comes back to us. The Amplified Bible says it like this:

> *Be careful what you are hearing. The measure* [of thought and study] *you give* [to the truth you hear] *will be the measure* [of virtue and knowledge] *that comes back to you—and more* [besides] *will be given to you who hear* (Mark 4:24).

When the writer of Proverbs explained how to influence and guard our hearts, he said:

My son, give attention to my words; incline your ear to my sayings. Do not let them depart from your eyes; keep them in the midst of your heart....Let your eyes look straight ahead, and your eyelids look right before you. Ponder the path of your feet, and let all your ways be established (Proverbs 4:20-21, 25-26).

God spoke to Joshua through Moses and said:

This Book of the Law shall not depart from your mouth, but you shall meditate in it day and night, that you may observe to do according to all that is written in it. For then you will make your way prosperous, and then you will have good success (Joshua 1:8).

This was God's instruction for becoming the kind of leader people would follow.

Paul gave the church at Philippi the recipe for victory when he said:

Finally, brethren, whatever things are true, whatever things are noble, whatever things are just, whatever things are pure, whatever things are lovely, whatever things are of good report, if there is any virtue and if there is anything praiseworthy—meditate on these things (Philippians 4:8).

Maybe the psalmist said it best:

Blessed is the man...[whose] delight is in the law of the Lord, and in His law he meditates day and night. He shall be like a tree planted by the rivers of water, that brings forth its fruit in its season, whose leaf also shall not wither; and whatever he does shall prosper (Psalm 1:1-3).

To *meditate* means "to ponder, consider, think on or imagine." One of the Old Testament Hebrew words for meditate means, "to mutter over and over, or to frame up." Too often the English translation loses the original meditative implication in many very simple words and phrases like "waiting on the Lord," "considering," or "thinking."

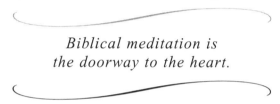

*Biblical meditation is
the doorway to the heart.*

Biblical meditation is the doorway to the heart. As a person meditates, he ponders and considers God's Word, God's presence, or even a particular problem that needs to be solved. By focusing inward (reducing the mental clutter and outward focus), we begin to hear with the ears of the heart. Meditation focuses us on the present, where we experience the presence of God. Through meditation, we experience God's Word, God's presence, and God's promise, and they become real in our hearts.

One of the greatest things that happens as we ponder, consider, and meditate on the reality of Christ in us is that we become aware of who we really are. We enter the realm of being and leave addition and subtraction behind.

Every person lives and performs out of a sense of self. Knowing and experiencing who you are in Jesus catapults you into high performance without having to achieve.

Start the process today with these steps:

1. Write out a scripture that describes who you are in Jesus. Pick one that has an attribute you would

desire to add if you were using math instead of miracles.

2. Memorize that scripture.

3. Close your eyes and create a mental picture of you functioning with that trait active in your life.

4. Ponder it until you feel the emotions you would feel by living in that character trait.

5. Now acknowledge to God, "Because Christ is in me and I am in Him, this is who I am. I have the power to live this life."

6. Repeat these exercises until this becomes your reality.

CHAPTER TWENTY

THE IMAGINARY ME

Coming to grips with eternal realities can be more than the mind wants to deal with! It defies a way of thinking that we've spent a lifetime perfecting. Looking beyond the world of the five senses to accept God's reality is one of the greatest acts of faith you will ever consider. But this very issue will determine whether you spend the rest of your life vainly attempting to fix the imaginary you or accepting the new you who is filled with resurrection life and power!

Our mind is the great battlefield of life. It is the arena of the grand conflict for identity. This is where new life explodes into our consciousness, becoming the realization of the promises of God. Or, it's where our new identity is buried in the illusion of "the imaginary me." We have trained our mind to be so finely attuned to the natural senses that we readily notice every subtle indicator that comes from the external world. We accept the input of the five natural senses without question. Our mind is schooled to accept all the natural indicators that sustain the illusion of the old man while pretending to become our new man.

A great philosopher once said, "I think, therefore, I am." As wonderful as that sounds, it produces a misconception. It creates the idea that "I am my thoughts." Thoughts may reveal who I am in character, but they don't necessarily reflect my true identity. Thoughts can be realistic illusions that take me into a world that only exists on my mindplane. Thoughts can create images so strong and clear that I can't tell the difference between the illusion and the reality.

Studies indicate that the mind knows no difference between a real event and something clearly imagined. Thus the physiology is affected by thoughts whether real or imagined. This is why the apostle John said, *"Beloved, I pray that you may prosper in all things and be in health, just as your soul prospers"* (3 John 2). The rest of our being cannot prosper if our soul does not prosper. The way we think and feel will only prosper if we grasp God's truth about who we are in Jesus as our reality. Our perception of who we are in Christ must be so strong that it becomes the way we think and feel about ourselves!

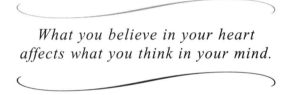

What you believe in your heart
affects what you think in your mind.

Thoughts are more than the input from our five senses. All of our thoughts are processed through the beliefs of our heart. The heart is the place where our sense of self is created and sustained. The two main sources of thoughts are memories from the past or imaginations of the future. When remembering the past, we never stop at remembering just the facts. We remember all past events the way we interpret them based on our sense of self.

Likewise, when thinking forward, we create an imagination of the future based on our self-perception. These mental movies become our road maps to the future. If those dreams are based on our old sense of self, we will limit our future to the experience of our past. This is why Jesus said, when teaching about the heart, *"For whoever has, to him more will be given; but whoever does not have, even what he has will be taken away from him"* (Mark 4:25). Unless we change our heart through the Word of God, we simply get more of what we've had.

The transformation process is not about becoming a new person. Transformation is about allowing the true you to emerge. It is not about becoming—it is about being. Believing that you're the old you trying to become the new you causes you to act like the old you. You will feel like the old you! You will struggle with the same issues as the old you! All of this becomes false indicators that Jesus did not really make you a new creation. Losing the battle in your mind limits your ability to experience the new you!

Believe it or not, there is a new righteous, powerful, confident, empowered person just waiting to explode into your consciousness. This person is not who you are trying to become—it's who God created you to be at your new birth! You are not trying to become this person—you are this person...now! The war for your identity is waged in your mind. How you see yourself becomes the life that you experience.

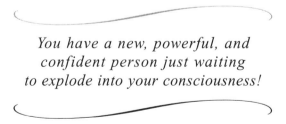

You have a new, powerful, and confident person just waiting to explode into your consciousness!

All the writers of the New Testament clearly express that our warfare is not with the devil. The devil is a defeated foe. Struggling with the devil is like struggling with our old man. Paul said it was like beating the air or shadow boxing. We are giving our attention to a powerless image that was defeated by the resurrected Lord. No, our warfare takes place on a battlefield much closer to home than the heavens. This war takes place in our mind! Paul explained that our battle was with vain imaginations that usurp God's realities.[1]

Our lusts, according to Peter, war in our soul.[2] The word *lust* simply means "desire." Desire is not sin. God knows we have desires, and He wants to fulfill them in a way that won't destroy us. When we have desires, our sense of identity will determine how we try to fulfill those desires. If you believe you're still the old you, then the way you try to find fulfillment will be based on your old identity. If you have a sense of the righteous you in Jesus, you will turn to God to find biblical, godly ways to satisfy your desires.

When you find yourself caught between living like the old you and the new you, then you start the war in your mind for identity. After you have fulfilled your desires in an ungodly manner you feel guilt. And you may even think God is making you feel the guilt. But He isn't! God doesn't use guilt to bring about transformation—He uses truth. What you are experiencing is an attack of conscience.

The word *conscience* means "dual knowledge." You have two sources of knowledge: the outer world and the inner world. When the voice of your natural man conflicts with the voice of God in you, the result is a feeling of guilt.

---

1. 2 Corinthians 10:5, KJV: *"Casting down imaginations, and every high thing that exalteth itself against the knowledge of God, and bringing into captivity every thought to the obedience of Christ."*

2. 1 Peter 2:11: *"Beloved, I beg you as sojourners and pilgrims, abstain from fleshly lusts which war against the soul."*

God is not condemning you. Guilt is the proof that your new righteous nature is no longer compatible with sin!

God is convicting and persuading you of sin, righteousness, and judgment.[3] He does not convict of sin by pointing out your sins. He convicts of sin by calling us to believe in Him and His finished work. He convicts of righteousness by His resurrection from the dead. He convicts of sin because the ruler of this world has been judged. The voice of the Spirit says to us, "You can get up. You are righteous. You can conquer this problem." The voice of our natural mind says, "No! I am the old me. I have these problems. They are stronger than I am." When these two sources of knowledge are in conflict, we experience guilt.

Our mind and emotions say, "You have to win the war." Jesus in us says, "I have won the war." Our body says, "That sin is too powerful." Jesus says, "Sin has no power over you." Our self-image says, "I must become righteous." The resurrection of Jesus says, "You are righteous." The illusion says, "You must win the battle." The cross says, "The battle is won." As the prophet Isaiah asked, *Whose report will you believe?"*

Paul said we must bring every thought captive to the obedience of Christ. In other words, we must put every thought, every emotion to the test of the resurrection by asking, "Are my thoughts, opinions, and ideas consistent with what Jesus accomplished by His obedience to death, burial, and resurrection?" If my view conflicts with the finished work of Jesus, I must reject it totally. Whether I do or do not understand it, I cannot accept as my reality any point of view that contradicts the finished work of Jesus. Like every illusion, it will dissipate as I place my attention elsewhere!

---

3. See John 16:8-10.

Our natural reasoning says, "This is real! Because I feel this in my body, it must be the truth." How many times have you had a worrisome thought? You experience stomach pains. The processes of all your bodily functions change. Your heart rate speeds up. You begin to perspire. The things that are happening in your body are real, but they are the physiological reactions to something that is not true. As soon as you discover that the bad news is not true, relief comes. The physiological changes were simply the results of what you believed to be true!

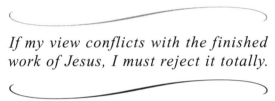

If my view conflicts with the finished work of Jesus, I must reject it totally.

Whatever we accept as our reality causes physiological and neurological changes to take place in our body. It changes the way we think, react, and behave. Each belief has the power to fulfill its own image. The more you see yourself as your new man, the more you experience the power to be who you really are in Christ!

Remember, there is an imaginary you. This person once was you. This person's life once was the life you lived. But that person, that "you," is now dead. That person only exists in your memories. That person was crucified with Christ. There is now a new you, a new creation. This new you is the reality!

Changing the way you think starts with a decision, a choice. Follow these steps to put the new you into action.

1. Decide to believe the truth about you in Jesus.
2. Then discover the information you will use to determine who you really are.

3. Develop a strategy for how you will react when internal conflict arises.

4. Make a list of opinions that you have about you.

5. All the ones that are in opposition to Jesus' finished work mark with a big red "X."

6. Pray and commit your intention to the Lord.

CHAPTER TWENTY-ONE

THE FUTURE IS NOW

In the early 1970s, I knew in my heart that writing would be the way I would have the greatest influence on the world. I was sure I would write and distribute books to the nations of the world. At that time, however, writing was my weakest skill. I had no one to teach me, and I had no connection or resources for distribution. It looked as if it would be very far in the future.

A few years later, I became good friends with a man who had written several very successful books. One day I shared my dream. "I know I'm going to write as a major part of my ministry!"

"What are you working on right now?" was his instant reply.

"Well, nothing yet, I don't..."

Before I could finish, he interrupted me and said, "You're not going to be a writer!"

"No," I insisted, "I'm really serious about this."

After several minutes of challenging banter, he finally said, "If you were *going* to write, you would be writing. Either you are a writer or you aren't."

I learned the lesson my friend was driving home. "Going to" usually never happens. Either we are or we aren't. If we are, we live like we are right now. As bad as they were, I began writing manuscripts that week. Taking that step ended my illusion that my lack of past training could limit me. By taking action, I brought the future into the present. Anyone can do this. We must live in the eternal now! The past is over. The future is a myth. There is only now. I realized I could be a writer or I could *become* a writer. If I chose to become, who knows what type of hindrances I would unnecessarily place on myself? What imaginary limitation would I create?

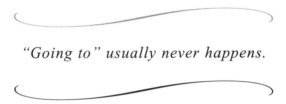

"Going to" usually never happens.

Today I have published dozens of books and workbooks for millions of people. All it took was starting...and being! Starting unlocks a hidden door to the heart. There are many people who confess or "affirm" all the right things. Their self-talk is pretty good. But they still never start. Then they wonder why this biblical concept doesn't work.

When there is a contradiction between the verbal and non-verbal communication, we always believe the non-verbal. This rule not only applies to your observation of others, but it's also the way you respond to yourself. When what you say is not aligned with your actions, you don't believe what you say. The disparity corrupts your heart and soon your own words have little value or meaning to you.

Jesus said:

Whoever says to this mountain, "Be removed and be cast into the sea," and does not doubt in his heart, but believes that those things he says will be done, he will have whatever he says (Mark 11:23).

Jesus didn't say that you must believe God's words are true. He said you must believe that your words are true. When our actions do not align with our words, we lose the value of our words. Our heart will not release the grace of God into our lives.

People who believe they *"are"* are not only taking action today, but they also value those actions, no matter how small. People who are trying to *become* get frustrated when their actions are not large enough. They are looking to the ultimate results from their actions to prove they *are!*

Today I am the president of a college that prepares students for ministry. I have watched thousands of students come and go over the last twenty years. Without exception, the ones who are *going* into the ministry never do. The ones who see themselves as ministers now will nearly always live their dream. Because they *"are,"* they align every aspect of their life with their sense of identity.

You can't really *become*—you can only be. The person who is becoming will have a demarcation point at which they will believe they are. When they reach that goal, they've got to accept that they *"are."* Usually they go out and get a job doing what they want to do. In the doing, they are affirmed that they *"are."* But if they ever lose the opportunity to do, they no longer feel they *"are."*

Several years ago, I left the ministry for a year. I never felt differently about myself. I led people to Jesus. I counseled. I did all the things that I would have done if I had been in a ministry job. Many times I was asked if I missed being a minister. I could only reply, "I never stopped being a minister. I just stopped pastoring a church." I have seen people step out of their "field" and never get back in. During the time they took off, they lost their sense of identity, for it was all based on doing.

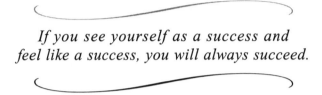

If you see yourself as a success and feel like a success, you will always succeed.

The person who sees himself as a success and feels like a success will always succeed. You can't take it away from him. If he loses everything he has, he will get it again; he can't help it. It is more than what he does. It is who he is. Proverbs says it like this: *"For a righteous man may fall seven times and rise again, but the wicked shall fall by calamity"* (Proverbs 24:16). Righteousness and wickedness are heart issues. Both will follow the course of the heart. The righteous man may fall, but he gets up. The wicked man may do good, but he falls.

This is more than mere positive thinking. This is about how you see yourself. It's about drawing upon and releasing the power of God to be who you really are in Jesus. Your future will be the result of what you do and the decisions you make now. If you see yourself as poor and you feel poor, the next decision you make will be the decision a poor person would make. If you see yourself as successful, the next decision you make will be the decision a successful person would make. There is no escaping who you believe you are.

I have spent years developing my Heart Physics® program. Very early in my walk with God, I realized that the heart was the secret to living in limitless power. It was the place that God chose to commune with man. It was the seat of all we are. I knew that if I was to understand life, I must understand the heart.

When I discovered that the Bible taught us to guard, guide, and write on our heart, I realized that I could program my destiny by how I influenced my heart. My ministry to me is the ministry to my heart. After speaking of the benefits of God's Word and of walking in peace and mercy, the writer of Proverbs said, "...*Write them on the tablet of your heart*" (Proverbs 3:3). I realized that knowing God's Word and having it written on my heart were two totally different things. Information was intellect. Heart beliefs were true power, good or bad. Writing on the heart affects the fabric of our being. Information only changes what we know. It gives us new goals without the power to get there.

The heart is only influenced by what is perceived as present tense. God lives in the eternal now, and He has designed us to live in the eternal now. All affirmations, whether verbal or non-verbal, should be positive, personal, and present tense. Instead of saying to myself "I will be wealthy one day," I would emphasize God's present tense promises: "I am successful and prosperous. I have the capacity for wealth." Each of these scripture-based present-tense affirmations emphasizes the present. When making such acknowledgments, I would involve my emotions and my imagination to make them come alive to me. The combination of left-brain, right-brain activity is the fast track to writing on the heart! This would make me what James called the poetic performer.

In making an affirmation personal, it can't be "us" or "we." It must be "me" and "I." I must create a sense of "me" when I am acknowledging or meditating on God's promises. It can't be general. It is about me. It is not about what God will do in the future. It has to be about me experiencing God's Word now!

The first rule for influencing the heart is that all affirmation and meditation must be positive. The focus cannot be on the problem or obstacle you want to overcome. It must be on the solution. The thought, "I'm not going to eat as much today," is focused on the problem. It is pushed to the future. It says what I am not going to do, therefore, it is negative. The more proper way to do this would be to acknowledge, " I am easily satisfied. I only eat small portions." Or, "I am strong and healthy. My body only desires fresh nutritious foods. Wholesome, nutritious food satisfies my hunger."

Preparing for the future is found in the subtlety of being. Back in my college days, I saw myself as a minister of the Gospel. Therefore, when I dressed every morning, I dressed like a person who accepted his responsibility as a leader. I didn't think about it. I just did it. Some of my classmates dressed as casually as the rules would allow. They saw themselves as students becoming ministers. They held to the idea that they would be in the ministry someday. Dressing like a minister would be put off until then. But when opportunity came knocking, it didn't notice them. On the other hand, opportunity always found me.

While I was in school, I was invited to speak in the main services of our church, something that rarely ever happened for a student. I had several personal meetings with the president of the college. I was invited to go on ministry trips with some of the staff. Doors opened for me with no effort on my part. In fact, Proverbs says that when you write God's Word on your heart, the result will be favor.

"And so find favor and high esteem in the sight of God and man" (Proverbs 3:4).

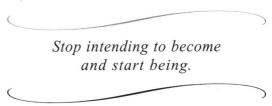

Stop intending to become
and start being.

End your intention to become. Start being! Very often when training leaders who are struggling, I make this request: "Tell me who you are apart from telling me what you do." It is rare that they know what to say, hence the root of their struggle. You will enjoy and value every step you take toward your goal if you believe you are. It's like the difference between inheriting the perfect piece of property or driving out to consider buying the piece of dream property. If you're considering it, you worry about the cost. You become anxious as you make the drive. What if someone else has made an offer? What if the down payment is too much? What if…what if…what if?

On the other hand, if you have inherited the property, you don't have a care in the world. The drive is pleasant. All the flowers stand out, and the sky looks brighter. You're not concerned with delays. You are just excited about what is yours.

Are you ready to be your future? Follow these steps to begin your transformation.

1. Begin to monitor your self-talk.
2. Does it reflect being or becoming?
3. Is it positive, personal, and present tense?
4. Choose an area of negative self-talk. Make a written list of how you intend to talk to yourself on index cards.

5. Every time you catch yourself talking negatively, interrupt the thought and replace it with new self-talk.

6. Start every day with healthy self-talk that you commit to the Lord.

7. Find scriptural promises that support your new self-talk.

8. Always acknowledge that you are a new creation.

CHAPTER TWENTY-TWO

THE END FROM THE BEGINNING

By now you have learned what few people will ever discover. The secret you've discovered was at one time an eternal mystery. This reality of the Gospel was beyond the knowledge of any Old Testament believer. This mystery, this secret, this reality is the power of *being*!

The new unlimited you is fully formed on the inside. At the new birth, your spirit was made new and empowered by the presence of God. Christ came to dwell in you by the Holy Spirit. Internally you have become all you'll ever need to be to live all of the promises of God!

Now it is time for you to access the power! Don't try to get it. Don't try to become...just simply access the real you, the you that *"was created according to God, in true righteousness and holiness"* (Ephesians 4:24). The apostle Paul, in that same verse, explained how so simply: You just put him on! You don't get the power to live the abundant life—you access it.[1]

Now it is time for you to decide what your future will be. Some argue, "No, shouldn't I wait for God to do that?" Certainly, if God speaks to your heart or shows you something specific about your life, yield to His leadership. But

---

1. Romans 5:1-2: *"Therefore, having been justified by faith, we have peace with God through our Lord Jesus Christ, through whom also we have access by faith into this grace in which we stand, and rejoice in hope of the glory of God."*

until then, the choice is yours. The Bible promises He will give you the desires of your heart if you delight in Him!

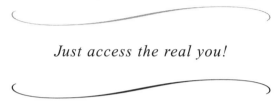

Just access the real you!

In Isaiah 46:10 God is described as *"Declaring the end from the beginning."* Because the new you has the mind of Christ and the nature of God, you too should declare your end from the beginning. Don't wait to see what the end will be. Decide what it will be. Make that decision based on the new you. Do so as if there were no limitations. In Christ all things are possible. The only boundaries are the ones you allow to remain in your own heart. Enter the realm of limitless living. Accept the promises of God as being real and being yours...*NOW!*

Every day that you live in the eternal now your outer world will harmonize with your inner world. The same power that transformed your inner man will permeate your outer man and your outer world!

Stay connected!

Never lose your sense of Christ in you. Stay connected to God in a way that empowers your life. Paul once said to the Galatians, *"Christ cannot help you"* (Galatians 5:2, NLT). They were saved, but they had left that place where Christ "in them" was able to affect their outer life. They had become unplugged from their power source.

Although we have *"all things that pertain to life and god-liness"* (2 Peter 1:3), even though all the promises of God are ours, we must live in this vital union with Christ where we feel His love and acceptance. We must remain sensitive to the Holy Spirit who will teach us to walk through life on these new terms. We must ever remain connected to God as our Source!

Strap on your seat belt. You are in for the ride of your life! Enjoy the journey.

ABOUT THE AUTHOR

D r. James B. Richards is best described in one word: *pioneer*. Since 1972 he has proclaimed a message that is practical, relevant, simple, safe, and empowering. Through his personal, innovative, and sometimes outrageous ministry style, millions of people around the world have been drawn into a loving relationship with God while finding love and restoration in their personal relationships.

A best-selling author and successful teacher, theologian, and businessman, Dr. Richards is in high demand as a speaker and personal advisor to business people, clergy, and political leaders. His personal process of emerging from years of pain, dysfunction, and deep bitterness has given him proven tools for success in life, ministry, and business. Although he holds degrees in theology, human behavior, and medicine, his teaching is simple, well-rounded, understandable, and easy to apply. The results have been proven in nearly thirty years of personal, professional, and clinical application.

Dr. Richards is also the Senior Pastor of Impact of Huntsville. IOH is a local church that has been built by reaching beyond the boundaries of the church to those who do not know Jesus. Through innovative outreach, interactive multimedia presentation of the Gospel, and an uncanny ability to connect with the lost, hundreds of people come to Jesus in services at Impact of Huntsville every year.

Today Dr. James B. Richards is still living out of that same passion that took him to the streets over thirty years ago. His message to the Church is simple: "When the world sees God in the Church, they will fill our auditoriums and want to know God."

Impact International School of Ministry

Impact International School of Ministry is raising up leaders who are able to meet the needs of this generation. The twentieth-century Church is out of touch with the real needs of society. We have become a sub-culture that speaks a language no one understands. Our methods are outdated and ineffective. We are answering the questions that no one is asking, while ignoring and minimizing the ones that are being asked.

We have become like the religious community of Jesus' day. We cling to our tradition and make the Word of God of no effect. More than once I have looked at ultra-religious people and applied this verse to them. The truth is, any method I cling to that is no longer effective has become my tradition.

Tradition comes from things that were good, from things that worked at one time. The Church is like the children of Israel who didn't want to worship in the temple because they still clung to the tabernacle. That was good, but its time had passed. God's life, presence, and power were no longer there. It was time to move on.

Several major sources tell us that the majority of Church growth in America is actually Christians going from one church to another. We are not really growing. The Church has become a marketing agency that competes for those who know Jesus while abandoning those who do not know Him.

Impact International School of Ministry will prepare you to reach this generation. Our commitment to the Word of God is absolute. Our commitment to methodology is as varied as the needs that exist. We are in touch with the world and we are on the cutting edge of what works.

If you are more interested in reaching the world than following the crowd, then this may be the training program for you. Impact International School of Ministry has a resident program and an external program through which you can earn a degree. For more information, contact:

Impact Ministries
3516 S. Broad Place
Huntsville, AL 35805
(256) 536-9402 ext. 301 Fax: (256) 536-4530
www.impactministries.com

Why Should I Choose Impact International School of Ministry?

I'm glad you asked!

1. **Evangelism**—IISOM was built on the power of one-on-one evangelism. Every student learns to win the lost and develop them into committed followers of Jesus.

2. **Missions**—Impact Ministries reaches millions of people around the world through its missions' efforts. Our students team up with some of the most powerful ministries in the world.

3. **Pastoral Training**—Jim Richards has spent nearly thirty years pioneering churches in America and around the world. You will have hands-on training and personal modeling from an entire staff that is committed to building the local church. You will be involved in the inner workings of a church that is effective at winning its city, is developing people, and has never had a split.

4. **Children's Ministry**—You will be trained in an innovative, positive children's ministry. If children are

your passion, you will be part of a children's ministry that is reaching kids.

5. **Youth and Teens**—Impact Ministries is in touch with the youth of our city. We speak their language, play their music, and minister to their needs. Train with people who are doing it, not just talking about it!

6. **Administration**—Be a leader who fulfills your vision! At IISOM learn how to organize, administrate, and build effective teams that work together for a cause. According to a recent study, this is a skill that few Christian leaders have ever developed.

7. **Counseling**—IISOM has powerful counseling programs that help people deal with the real issues of their heart instead of the continual cycle of rededicating and failing. If you want to counsel and really help people, you will never find a training opportunity like this!

8. **Substance Abuse**—The minister who cannot effectively work with substance abuse will not be effective in this generation. Learn from certified substance abuse counselors. Work in our substance abuse clinic with real users. Experience what it takes to get people clean and free in Jesus.

9. **Mentoring**—Do you want to spend the next two to four years sitting in a class with someone spouting theories or do you want to work alongside caring ministers who allow you to become involved? Mentoring makes the difference between theory and reality.

10. **A Real Church Environment**—IISOM is part of a real church that is active in the community. You will get to see how everything you learn in school is applied in a

real church environment. While you attend school you will have a church family that serves your family and sees you as more than a student.

11. **New Covenant Based Interpretation**—At IISOM you will study every page of the Bible from the perspective of faith righteousness, grace, peace, and the unconditional love of God. You will be established in the New Covenant, not a mixed message of law and works.

Impact International School of Ministry has a well-rounded program, caring teachers, and a proven track record. We do not specialize in one doctrine or one issue. We know it takes more than one strong point to build a ministry. We've covered all the bases. You will be ready to succeed in life and ministry!

You may be a person who knows you have a call from God, but doesn't know what it is. At IISOM you will be given the opportunity to find your place and discover your dreams. More importantly, you will be empowered to live them to the fullest. Because we teach all of our material in a way that applies to ministry, business, or personal life, it will be an investment in your future, your call, and your personal dreams.

Don't Wait Another Day! Enroll TODAY!
(256) 536-9402 ext. 301 — www.impactministries.com

BOOKS BY DR. JAMES B. RICHARDS

Leslie Fox
Cell phone 724-624-2010
e-mail loviemountain@comcast.net